AF363280

Samuel Vožeh

Why Do We Exist?

*A possible rational concept
and an incommodious personal
path to the answer*

Translated from German by Fabian Claus
Edited by Allison Turner

The English edition has been revised and supplemented with additional references.

Title of the German Edition: Warum gibt es uns Menschen? Eine mögliche rationale Erklärung und ein unbequemer persönlicher Weg zu einer Antwort. ISBN: 9783955292478

The proof of life is to live,

The proof of love is to love.

Contents

FOREWORD

The author of this text is an ordinary human being. *Ordinary* referring to the fact that I am no philosopher or writer. I am neither a spiritual teacher nor a monk. I am not a psychic with the ability to communicate with angels or other metaphysical entities. I am a husband, father of two, retired physician, scientist and psychotherapist. The book – which has as its main topic the spiritual dimension[1] of our existence as human beings – has been written for ordinary people too: women and men who are not on a quest for spectacular, esoteric experiences, salvific gurus or instructions from extra-terrestrials. This is a text for people who earnestly ask themselves the question 'Why do I live?' and seek to take responsibility for their own lives.

The author

PART I:
WHY DO HUMAN BEINGS EXIST?

IT COULD BE[*]

It could be – someone designed and created the world. This supernatural entity would need to possess the knowledge of an engineer – the knowledge of a bioengineer, in fact, since biology serves (from my point of view as a human being) as the most important factor within the existence of intelligent, conscious beings capable of self-reflection. It must have been a genius, with a grand knowledge of the creation of life out of inanimate matter. At the same time, it must have been someone with a good helping of humour – dark humour, even cynicism. Because, if someone had knowledge vast enough to create the world, he or she must have known of the suffering that would eventually be brought about. He or she must have had cognisance of the fact that the most intelligent being amongst those he/she called into existence would realise the absurdity of it all and see no possibility to emerge from it, to overcome it. Why had he or she created the whole? Perhaps as some sort of experiment. A very important experiment perhaps, which was meant to yield crucial results. (...)

---

[*] In place of an introduction, this book begins with an excerpt from an entry in a journal written more than ten years ago. Perhaps there are readers for whom the text will serve as a reminder of similar notions regarding the genesis and significance of *the whole* within which we live and find our being. The author asks the readers to bear with him, should they experience the tone of the journal entry as pretentious, cumbersome or irreverent.

It could be – the world came to existence by chance, by accident, 'durch Zufall', 'par hasard'. In that case, life would be happenstance. Born by chance out of a nothingness, or born out of something we cannot yet describe and understand – from a state preceding the very Big Bang referred to time and again. The Big Bang, by chance. The expansion of the universe, then, by chance. The galaxies and the solar system, the sun, by chance. The earth by chance. The composition, by chance, of matter on and surrounding the earth. The temperature conditions which made the emergence of life possible, by chance. The creation of organic molecules out of the elements, by chance. Small vesicles, by chance composed from proteins and lipids, vesicles that are separated from their surroundings by a mere partially permeable membrane. An assumption of the autonomy of these vesicles, i.e. an increase in the degree of organisation regarding the individual structures in relation to and at the expense of the surrounding structures, by chance. The capacity to duplicate and multiply, the emergence, by chance, of organisms progressively more highly organised up to the human being. The development of language, by chance. (...)

It could be – man is to be blamed for his own plight. Very much as all the religions known to me – and not merely the Judaeo-Christian religions in effect in our cultural sphere – suggest. According to the Bible, man is at fault due to the fact that he has gained the knowledge of good and evil. The fact that he has attained said knowledge is supposed to be his own fault as well, as he himself has sought after said awareness. Man believes himself to be at fault. He has always believed it, has literally clung to it, insomuch that, when someone came and claimed that man could be absolved of said iniquity and be cured of this malignant disease merely by believing that He, the Son of God, could turn every human being into a Son of God through faith, He was eliminated by man. He who was eliminated eventually 'outwitted' man in the end, since it was precisely His death that led to thousands and millions of people believing in this tale of salvation from guilt by the Son of God. (...)

It could be – the universe was created by the eternal being, as a living entity, as a sphere with a smooth, vacant surface. The surface or edge of this universe has, according to Plato's 'Timaeus', no contact with the being beyond this border, because this being is nothing. Not a matter, not a power, simply nothingness, always there and always the same. This is why at the edge of the universe – the very surface of this sphere – there is nothing needed which would require making contact with the outside world. The celestial bodies were placed into the universe by the creation of time, which they measure by means of their movements. Time was created as a reflection of eternity. As a result of time passing, eternity materialises and in turn becomes graspable for rational thought. According to the account of Timaeus, man is constituted of an immortal part, created by the eternal being from a remnant of the mixture used for the creation of the being called universe, and of a mortal part, created by the young gods who had been created before man by the eternal being. If, during his lifetime, man succeeds in mastering the innate emotions (love accompanied by lust and grief, fear and anger as much as their opposites) within his own body, he will return after death to a blissful life beneath the same star. Should he not become master of these emotions, then his life cannot be deemed righteous, and he is to be returned to a body at a lower evolutionary stage after death. (...)

It could be – the world, as told in the Bible, was created in six days. Perhaps God, before the Big Bang, created all the information that was needed for the evolution of the universe and the earth, using a 'preBigBangian' informatics tool. The creation of said information, contained within the cosmos, took six 'preBigBangian' days. A day's rest was needed after the creation to process the implementation of the information into a virtual system to be executed. This virtual world worked perfectly and is described by mythology as the original ideal state, such as paradise (according to scientific reports, the state before the Big Bang is not describable by means of any physical tool currently available to man; the only information to be found is of mythological or religious nature). After this achievement, God moved to materialise creation within space-time. The starting point proved to be the Big Bang, as is known to us. The materialised creation was everything but perfect. This imperfection was, however, already included within the information which God had created before the Big Bang, and thus according to plan. The whole thing now runs its course until redemption is found in love. There was no need for love in the virtual world, because everything worked perfectly within it. The end state, the salvation of the world, is once more going to be information. Spatiotemporal matter is going to dissolve, but, unlike the 'preBigBangian' virtual world, this new world – which has originated out of the deliverance from matter – is going to entail and ceaselessly continue to create love. (...)

It could be – man is born out of an all-embracing divinity that continues to live within him and to which he returns once his life in this world has run its course. This divinity is indeed defined by Jesus as the Father – that is to say, the Procreator – in the New Testament of the Bible. Every human being is thus a part of this divinity, or has a fraction of it inherent within himself as his predisposition to yearn for spiritual experiences and absolute truths. Maybe the code to this fraction of divinity is entailed in the 'junk' or noncoding DNA within the human genome that, according to scientific reports, constitutes more than 50 per cent of all the information contained in the genome and whose function or purpose is still (in April 2004) unknown.

19th of April 2004

MAN IS SEARCHING FOR A RATIONALLY COMPREHENSIBLE 'MEANING OF IT ALL'

Our mind has the ability to ask the question, why *all this*? Why? What is the meaning or purpose of my existence on this earth? What of the existence of other people and creatures? What of the existence of Earth and the entirety of the cosmos which in its expanse remains ungraspable?[2]

The human mind may be able to ask this question, but is paradoxically not able to find an answer for it. As poignantly expressed at the beginning of this text by means of the journal entry, we can conceive of any number of more or less probable scenarios to explain what caused the world to exist.[3]

That our mind cannot provide an answer to this question is also what the philosophers, the most talented thinkers amongst men, tell us. According to Bertrand Russell, one of the most influential philosophers of the twentieth century, the question of meaning separates the field of life from those fields where philosophy is capable of providing answers.[4] Ludwig Wittgenstein writes in his famous *Tractatus Logico-philosophicus*: 'The solution of the riddle of life in space and time lies outside space and time.'[5] That is, beyond the dimension in which logic and reason operate. And Albert Camus, another influential philosopher and a literature Nobel laureate, writes in his book *The Myth of Sisyphus* that, using his reason, man perceives the world and human life as absurd, because he does not receive an answer to his question concerning the meaning of his existence.

There are belief systems that provide a *meaning of it all*; for instance, the concept of reincarnation in Hinduism or the belief in heaven and hell in Christianity or Islam. While the stories on which they are based may represent logical constructions that are intelligible, the beliefs cannot be rationally justified by means of logical reasoning and objective facts. The beliefs are outside of what the mind is capable of explaining. This is why many sophisticated atheists and agnostics regard these stories as being invented by man in his need for the meaning of life.

A search for the purpose of this world we live in on a rational level, that is, deriving the answer based on objective evidence and logical thought, is doomed to failure. Man must seek an answer on another level. Indeed, many women and men find the deeper meaning of their existence by means of personal and first-hand experiences gained on a spiritual path. According to accounts reaching back to the very beginning of recorded history[6], there is a level to human existence – namely the spiritual level[7] – on which it is possible for human beings to find meaning in their existence.

However, even those who are no longer on the search for meaning – who have had a deep experience on another level – feel the need to define the reason for human existence in rational terms, even though this experience lies beyond reason and cannot be put into words.[8] For human beings, language represents the most important means of communication. And communication by means of language can only take place on a rational level. Bertrand Russell writes, 'For it is necessary to enlist reason in order to give an account of anything whatever.'[9] If we attempt to report on these experiences, we have to resort to a rational discourse level.

This could be seen as a possible explanation for the origin of religious teachings. In the beginning, there was a direct experience of something beyond man's grasp, something encompassing, something divine. To give an account of these experiences, to tell other people about them, had only been possible by means of a narrative, be it the story of Moses in the Old Testament, the tale of Krishna in the Bhagavad Gita or the stories of Jesus in the Gospels. The spiritual experiences also lead to the awareness of a deeper meaning of the totality of what we encounter as human beings in this world. This is why these stories contain a cosmology – an explanation of everything. They are different in every religion, as they reflect the cultural and social background of the time and place of their origin.[10]

Meanwhile, we discover that these attempts at communicating the experience of spiritual realities are not solely in the past. Important contemporary spiritual teachers and scholars too have the need to put said *totality*, which escapes rational reasoning, into a rationally comprehensible structure.

An example can be found in the important and useful concept of the evolution of consciousness, as it takes place in individuals from birth up to adulthood, and its analogy to the evolution of the consciousness of humankind as a whole, in the course of human history on this earth. This evolution from an archaic to an integral consciousness has been described by Jean Gebser in his work *Ursprung und Gegenwart*[11] and has further been integrated into and applied to Ken Wilber's cosmology.[12] The cosmology of Ken Wilber, who thinks of himself not as a spiritual teacher but more as a scholar and philosopher, does not merely explain the current state of the world we live in. It also predicts the further evolution toward an integral consciousness and describes ways in which this evolution can be nurtured. Based on his theory, Ken Wilber points towards a behaviour that is meant to have a positive effect on the evolution toward integral consciousness and analyses the actions of political figures with respect to positive behaviour. Ken Wilber's cosmology has furthermore provided the basis for currently active political movements and parties such as the *Integrale Politik* in Switzerland. His work is, in that sense, not only to be read as spiritual teachings or a *possible* cosmology but as an *ideology* that shows – for those who believe in it – the direction in which mankind has moved and is to continue moving.

Even important contemporary spiritual teachers have a concept they use to try to explain the epoch in which mankind finds itself and how it has developed and will further develop in spiritual terms. Suggestions corresponding to this notion are found in a book by the influential spiritual teacher Eckhart Tolle, titled *A New Earth*.[13] Willigis Jäger, one of best-known spiritual teachers in the German-speaking world, writes in his last book, 'It appears that a time of collective awakening has arrived. We are experiencing the beginning of a new age, of a revolution. We are discovering that man is more than a being defined by his intellect.' (Translated by the author)[14]

Some ideologies are intended to foster the formation of politically active organisations, but this need for a descriptive theory emanates instead from these teachers' desire to share their experiences with other people. They have walked a path that led them and many other women and men to an *awakening,* to an experience of all-encompassing love and the deeper meaning of the existence of man. This experience bears the wish for all human beings to take part in it. However, this path may be long and may entail difficult steps. To set forth and remain on this path requires powerful motivation. If the information on the path and its redemptive experience is embedded in a cosmological concept, then its appeal and the incentive to walk this path increases.

This aforementioned wish has motivated the creation of the text at hand: to tell a feasible story, which on a rational plane describes the *meaning of it all.* A story that not only makes sense but is also alluring and provides an incentive – a narrative on the birth of love on planet Earth. Love, not understood as a momentary idealisation connected to powerful emotions but as the deep awareness of being accepted, as an attitude of compassion, and as the unconditional acceptance of all people and beings.

Authentic spiritual experience is always connected to the experience of said love. We too find it – according to the Dalai Lama – as the core theme constantly present in all the different religions.[15] Krishnamurti, for whom the direct personal experience free from any kind of ideology or teaching was of utmost importance, says, 'There is no silence without love.'[16]

Today, love is considered an essential factor also in the fields of psychology and sociology. With regard to the mental health and integrity of individual people, it might just represent the most important basic need.[17] In his book *The Meaning of Life*, Terry Eagleton identifies love as the (only) possibility to reconcile 'our search for individual fulfilment' – unique to our species – with the fact that humans can only exist as social beings.[18] This is why he sees love as the focal point in the aftermath of a discussion of western philosophy spanning from the Greek to the postmodern age. Love is thus one of the greatest goods, if not the greatest good, even when considered on the rational plane.[19] It proves to be the starting point of the concept described in this text for *a possible* rationally comprehensible *meaning of it all.*

A POSSIBLE 'MEANING OF IT ALL'

As human beings, we realise that we nowadays find ourselves in this cosmos, on planet Earth, where many other beings reside. How this cosmos that surrounds us was formed, we do not know. Modern physics attempts to describe the processes that have led to the emergence of the material world in which we live, by way of complex theories and models.[20]

If we observe the cosmos with the resources currently at our disposal, we have to side with Jaspers in proclaiming that our existence – when compared to the size of the universe – takes place on a speck of dust.[21] Considered as pure matter, our Earth – and with it we, as individual humans and humanity as a whole – is a nonentity.

Is there a specific meaning graspable by the human mind – a reason for the origination of life on this 'speck of dust'?

What is life?

Viewed from the outside, objects which we call living organisms are characterised by their ability to differentiate between themselves and their surroundings and the fact that they give preference to themselves *at the expense* of their environment. In order to preserve the necessary conditions for life within the internal confines (homeostasis), living organisms discharge *harmful substances* into the environment and take in nutrients necessary for the metabolism. One could also say that a living organism distinguishes – on this material plane – between *good* and *evil*. The things that serve its existence are considered *good* and those that threaten it are *evil*.

This differentiation means that the living organism creates a disturbance in the equilibrium of the environment, which in turn creates a threat to other beings. This becomes evident with more highly evolved animals that have to feed on other living organisms – be it animals or plants – that in turn have to give their lives.[22] This basic characteristic of all living beings – self-preference at the cost of their surroundings – leads to the fact that most living organisms become sustenance for other creatures and have to give their lives for them. What we – as the most advanced being on earth – call life is thus inevitably connected to a focus on the self. Without said separation from the surroundings, without this favouring of the self at the expense of the surrounding environment – in other words without the struggle with and the destruction of animate and inanimate things – living beings, as we know them, could not exist.

The most advanced being possesses the greatest destructive force

We all know and experience – at times very painfully – that this innate destructive force existing in every living entity is at its most developed with human beings. Due to their superiority, human beings are able to either successfully fight other creatures posing a threat to them or make use of other living beings for themselves. Man owes his superiority predominantly to his mind. With his mind, he is able to comprehend highly complex correlations between cause and effect, and to use this knowledge to exercise control over his surroundings.

Human beings also have a self-awareness that is closely connected to the capacity of the mind to think. The self reproduces, as it were, on an *immaterial* mental plane, the egocentrism and the *favouring of the self* that we find in every being on a material and instinct level. In this mental dimension, the egocentrism knows no limits. We want to have everything and exert as much power over our surroundings and fellow humans as possible.[23] This favouring of the self leads to an unstoppable, constant acceleration of the destruction of the environment and the use of violence against our own species.

Man seems to be caught up in this egocentrism. Even though we are able to rationally relate to the fact that this destruction will ultimately turn against us, we cannot put a stop to its growth. Perhaps the reason we do not manage to do so is that our egocentrism stems from the basic drive present in every living organism and, thus, in life itself: favouring of the self at the expense of the environment. The most advanced form of life, thus, also entails the most advanced stage of self-centredness and with it the greatest potential for destruction and the biggest threat for Earth and its inhabitants.

Consciousness, freedom and responsibility

We are aware of ourselves as humans within this cosmos, because we are equipped with a consciousness able to reflect on itself. It is not only a simple self-reflection, like recognising oneself in a mirror. The self-awareness of human beings reaches much deeper. We reflect on our past and anticipated future actions and *judge* them according to their consequences. We also know when we act in the awareness of the consequences, and *judge* ourselves as behaving *well or badly* and feel responsible for it. Following this, we are capable of asking the ultimate question: "Who am I?"

This ability to consciously perceive things – and in turn one's self – as an individual, i.e. from the perspective of the self, on one hand entails an ever-increasing egocentrism. On the other hand, it results in the fact that human beings are not entirely driven by their drives (i.e. hunger, aggression, sexual drive). They also have the freedom to not do something their drives or instincts dictate. They are able to decide between what they do or don't do.

As a consequence of this ability, man thus enters into a *conscious relationship* with his environment, i.e., is able to assume different attitudes. He may meet other beings with fear and aggression as a manifestation of his egocentrism that is shaped by his drive for survival, which is equally reciprocated. Every human being is alternatively able to enter a relationship where he meets his counterpart with compassion and caring acceptance, which he also receives in turn.

When entering a relationship with their environment, human beings also perceive suffering: the suffering that is a consequence of destruction and death, and thus inevitably a consequence of life. We are able not only to observe suffering in others, but also to feel pity for others, to suffer vicariously through them, very much as the blues musician, Tampa Red, poetically expresses in his song: 'When things go wrong, go wrong with you, it hurts me too.' Every human being has the ability to experience stirrings of love at the sight of suffering.

As human beings, we have the need – at least deep inside – to love and be loved in return. Not just in connection with reproduction and the welfare of one's offspring in mind, but due to our self-reflective consciousness capable of compassion.

We thus notice on an *individual level*, that every adult human being has acquired an ego and a strongly developed egocentric drive. On the other hand, we notice that the same human being holds – as a self-aware individual – within himself the seed out of which love can grow.

On the *level of the origin and the evolution of life on earth* we are analogously able to observe a similar process. Life, which entails suffering (the more highly advanced, the more suffering and potential for destruction and violence), in the emergence of human consciousness – the most advanced stage of development – also entails the capacity for love.

According to recorded history, the experience and living of love, originally proclaimed by Buddha and Christ as compassion and unconditional acceptance, was only possible for beings that had developed a sort of consciousness that is, as far as we know, possible only in humans.[24] Without this consciousness, love would have to remain an instinct. The conscious self that is able to decide what to do and not do is also necessary in order to set forth on the path that according to Christ and Buddha[25] leads to this experience.

The development of this consciousness in human beings was thus a necessary condition for the ability to receive this love as a gift and to pass it on to others, to love others out of freedom. Just as egocentrism signifies suffering and discontent for the individual, the environment and the world, love creates happiness and peace.

Whoever has experienced this love has experienced the ultimate purpose of human existence. These men and women feel blessed in an unprecedented way; they experience unlimited grace. After this experience, they know deep inside – without having to put it into words or thoughts – that they never again have to ask the question about the meaning of their existence. With this experience, their lives are fulfilled. They understand why all human beings who have witnessed this view love as the greatest good there is. They continue to live on in order to share the experience of this greatest good – the living of love – with as many people as possible.

In light of the authentic reports about these individuals, this experience and living of love is not a myth or a hypothesis, but a discernible reality with regards to the personal experiences and objectively verifiable observation of the behaviour and actions of these figures.[26]

A *possible* concept of the *meaning of it all* can be deduced from these observations and from our knowledge of the typical characteristics of living organisms and the history of the development of life on this earth. This concept is comprehensible on a rational plane, i.e. even to those people who have not experienced this love themselves. It is based on observable facts and does not make any use of unverifiable hypotheses.

The concept

From a present-day perspective, the experience and living of all-encompassing love has emerged on this earth at the end of a very long evolutionary process.[27] This is a possible answer to the question 'Why do we exist?' For people who have experienced this love, it is *the* answer, and for many – if not most – people without this personal experience, love – unconditional acceptance and compassion – is one of the greatest goods they know of. The birth and existence of love became possible in this world because of the emergence of life. Life, from the lowest evolutionary stage, brings suffering with it.

We do not know if, at the very start of these processes that led to the creation of the universe and life on earth, the birth and life of love on this planet had been intended as their goal. Neither do we know if the processes, which in some people lead to this birth, require the action of powers or energies not materially discernible by us (i.e. God) – powers that lie outside our corporeal shells. It is entirely possible that the ability to experience all-encompassing love is inherent in every man and woman. This is not of importance to the concept in question, since the latter does not touch upon the question of the existence of a power that guides the evolution.[28] This does not contradict the many narratives on which the different religions are based. It merely implies that the knowledge – based on our reason – in this case falls short. Note that by avoiding statements about these questions the concept avoids applying an unprovable hypothesis.

In addition to the question concerning the existence of a god of whom we could 'make ourselves an image', the presented concept for the possible *meaning of it all* leaves out the further evolution of life and consciousness on this earth. The notion that it has led to the miracle of the blossoming of freely lived love on Earth suffices as the *meaning of it all*. In other words, it does not see fulfilment in a more or less distant future, but in the present. Now, today, love – the greatest good that man knows of – is born every day, every hour, every moment, anew. Leaving open the question of further evolution means that this concept does not represent an ideology: it makes no recommendations on how human beings are supposed to act in order to guide world history into a specific direction.

The concept is based on facts clearly perceptible by all human beings and establishes a connection between the following:

1. The emergence of suffering as a necessary component of life as we know it and the increase of suffering as a result of the ego of man – the most highly advanced living creature.

2. The ability of this highest form of life to experience love as the greatest good and to share love. The perpetual blossoming of said love in women and men of various epochs and cultures, who carry it further during their lifetimes.

The concept is a possible answer to the question 'Why do we exist?' It is beautiful, because it regards the realisation of the greatest good there is as the purpose of human existence. Even so, it does not embellish the reality of life on earth.

As shown in the previous chapter, no proof that a possible concept is *the* answer can exist on the rational plane. A definite certainty can only be obtained on the personal level: by experiencing the all-encompassing love, an experience that cannot be comprehended by means of logical reasoning.

We can, however, use reason to ask how probable it might be that the answer is the right one. Like with Pascal's wager,[29] we can then weigh the odds, the losses and the gains, of believing it or dismissing it. Assuming, by means of the arguments listed above, that the answer the concept provides is correct, the meaning of our existence on this earth is found in the emergence and living of love. Thus, if a human being sought to fulfil the meaning of his or her existence in this world, his or her ultimate aspiration ought to be to experience and live this love. Alongside the reflections suggested in Pascal's wager we can ponder the odds of whether the hypothesis described in this text may be correct and the losses if it is correct and we dismiss it.

The concept may thus possibly encourage individual human beings to set forth on a personal path that leads to the experiencing of this greatest good and the *meaning of it all.* In that way, it might potentially contribute to more peace and less hatred in interpersonal relationships. The behaviour of individual people and the impact of that behaviour is however not a part of the concept at hand. Rather, this behaviour arises almost of its own accord when human beings have this experience.

The concept does not deny history or the fact that, in our time, many more people are able to walk this path than did a couple of thousand years ago. Buddha, Jesus and other individuals of antiquity and the Middle Ages can be compared – following Eckhart Tolle[30] – to the first emergence of a new kind of blossoming plant at a time when environmental conditions would not allow for their growth on a large scale. Today, because far more people are individually aware of their own existence and their freedom and responsibilities, the path to the personal experiencing of the greatest and most valuable good is accessible to more people. This development is, however, not an essential part of the concept.

As the author, I do not intend to conceal that this book is also an appeal. I would like to personally invite the reader to walk the path whereon countless women and men have found this love. Part II of this book describes this path. Perhaps, some readers might choose this path knowing the important privilege claimed by human beings living in our time: the privilege of having the freedom to decide and the awareness of the responsibilities that we humans have due to our existence.

After having read this text some may feel that the realisations presented herein do not represent anything innovative and do not do justice to the complexity of the subject matter – that the proposed concept was to present truisms that highly simplify the incomprehensible reality of the existence of man. This objection has merit. However, it does not change the fact that this concept offers a possible, rationally plausible and meaningful explanation of the human existence.

Finally, our mind could object that the same objective could have been reached without suffering, without the progression of the self-centred ego. The answer can only be silence. We do not know this. We can only bow in awe of the infinitely vast suffering of mankind in this world.

Concept Summary

The question of why we humans exist cannot be answered on a rational level, as a logical deduction based on observable and objectively verifiable facts. On an intellectual level, the search for meaning remains fruitless. Opposing this are the authentic accounts of spiritual experiences of many people according to which the lives of these people were suffused with meaning. These experiences have the immediate awareness of an all-engrossing love in common. The knowledge of being loved, of being kept in unconditional love and of not being able to help but to pass this love on to everyone else. For these people, this experience surpasses everything else that they have lived or were able to imagine. Their life is thereby given a deeper meaning, independent from the extent of suffering which it entails or has entailed. Assuming that it is rationally plausible to view love (the unconditional acceptance and compassion) as the greatest good there is, then a possible concept for the *meaning of it all* can be formulated. The text at hand attempts to show that the receiving and giving of love requires a consciousness, as we know it, in human beings. A necessary requirement for the formation of this consciousness was, on the other hand, the emergence of life and of planet Earth (which carries this life). This yields a possible explanation for the existence of *it all*, which is based on verifiable observations and rationally comprehensible arguments. According to the observations made, it is a plausible supposition that life in the form we know was not possible without suffering. Based on this supposition, a rationally comprehensible reason for the suffering can be postulated. Moreover, we can observe that suffering creates stirrings of compassion and affection and thereby possibly even directly contributes to the experiencing and living of love.

PART II:
THE PATH

Object-Free Meditation

Object-free meditation is not *the* way, but *a* way to the experience of the spiritual dimension[31]. It is a narrow, long and at times very arduous path.

Why this specific path and not another? Object-free meditation is at the heart of many different spiritual schools and has proven to be a successful spiritual path for many people over thousands of years.[32] It has been taught as Anapanasati in the Buddhist tradition,[33] represents a significant part of mindfulness yoga,[34] was practised by Desert Fathers and has been an element of Christian mysticism from the Middle Ages[35] until today.[36] Also, the awareness of breathing meditation, as described in the following instructions, constitutes a central practice in mindfulness-based psychotherapy.[37]

Yet, none of these reasons for exactly this path to be presented here is the crucial one. It is important to the author to recommend a path that he knows from personal experience. Many spiritual teachers – and probably all of those who are serious and authentic – have, over the course of many years, walked a path that led through difficulties, before they were able to find the answers they were looking for. However, some of their teachings say nothing of this very arduous path, but just invite people to share their fruit with them. As if it were possible – by listening to a talk, taking one or several courses or reading a book – to reach the same place without undertaking this long journey oneself.

With this remark, the author by no means seeks to cast doubt on the eminently grand value of courses and books by important spiritual teachers. He would merely like to clearly voice that he herein describes a path which he has not merely conceived of based on his knowledge from books or reports but walked himself. He is thus able to recommend it to others by virtue of first-hand experience. Therefore, the information found in this Part is largely based on personal experiences. The author has been able to gain these experiences in the course of ten years during a sort of shadow existence. This *shadow existence* took place alongside the ordinary everyday life everyone knows – job, family, work, holidays, celebrations and mourning. It was based on his devoting one to two hours every morning – and on most days an additional hour over lunchtime – to object-free meditation.

WHAT IS OBJECT-FREE MEDITATION?

The *knowledge* imparted by object-free meditation is independent of a concept or a specific dogma. It cannot be gained on the rational plane – by means of words. It is based on direct experience. Ever since the beginning of recorded history, countless people from various cultures, regions and religions have given accounts of these experiences.

Object-free meditation is a path leading inward. A path leading to our actual self as human beings – contained in love. Every genuine spiritual path meets at this place. This is why the citation from the Dalai Lama referred to in Part I reads: 'Since love is at the core of all religions, we could speak of a universal religion of love.' [38]

Nor can it be any different. Every human being holds a place within ourselves where love can be experienced as the ultimate ground. Depending on teaching, religion or tradition, this place has been given different names. Lao Tzu terms it Wuji-nature[39] – which is attained by means of tai chi as a spiritual path – Buddhism denominates it Buddha-nature,[40] Christianity calls it Christ,[41] who is born and lives within ourselves.

Different religions describe differing ways – rituals, tenets, rules of life, physical exercises – that lead to the experience of this fundamental element. Object-free or non-object meditation is one of the oldest and most direct ways. It is independent from religious or spiritual concepts, but by all means compatible with them due to its long-lasting tradition within different religions.

Object-free meditation, as it is described in the next chapter, is in its most basic form a very simple exercise: Breathing is used as an anchor to gather the mind and to bring oneself into the present moment – the here and now. In spite of that, to regularly practise object-free meditation is nevertheless anything but effortless and easy. It is a long journey with many surprising and sometimes unpleasant revelations regarding oneself. It requires courage and strength to accept these insights and remain on the path.

Is object-free meditation an *ego trip* and an *escape from reality*? Viewed from the outside, the spiritual path of object-free meditation might appear to be just that. As human beings, we are all but incessantly self-centred – on an *ego trip*. Be it to empower our ego, to protect it or to pursue desires. Frequently, these motivations remain unknown to us; for example, we may help other people in an attempt to feel like a better human being than others. In that sense, the motivation to practise object-free meditation can stem from the desire of the ego to be superior to other people in terms of a spiritual path – a desire, perhaps, for enlightenment and perfection by means of transcendental experiences. These desires are usually present in everyone who undergoes this journey.

On the way, we do realise that the path leads to a surprise for the ego. By means of regular practice, our ego becomes more transparent – we recognise it for what it really is: A bundle of stories, images and emotions with which we identify ourselves. The more clearly we see this, the more this identification dissolves. Object-free meditation could, in that sense, be described as a *paradoxical ego trip*: Even though the motivation often primarily stems from our ego, it itself – in a manner of speaking – cuts the branch on which it is sitting.

Another notion regarding the path of meditation – usually making people not want to set forth on it – can be found in the sentiment that it is some sort of *escape.* Does the meditating subject not flee from reality? Does he or she not engage in navel-gazing, constructing an idyllic world that does not resemble the reality of everyday life? It is indeed the case that many people turn to the spiritual path because they consciously or unconsciously regard it a means of escape from the reality of a life that overtaxes them. Yet, similarly to the *ego trip*, it constitutes a paradoxical escape, for the escape route comes to an end with reality. Regularly practising object-free meditation leads to a state where we see ourselves (our own reality), and also our surroundings (the reality within which we live) much more clearly and without any distortions. If the *ego trip* has been compared to the cutting of a branch on which the ego resides, then an escape on the path of object-free meditation could be compared to a boomerang whose flight comes to an end where it started.

It is in that place, where the identification with the ego ends and we are able to perceive of and accept reality without distortions, that we are able to experience and live with purpose, joy and love.

PRACTISING OBJECT-FREE MEDITATION

Where do I meditate?

With regards to the routine at home, you should arrange a space, as best you can, where you can meditate undisturbed. The easiest way to go about it is to place a mat or a blanket on the floor (for example, square with a side length of 30–40 inches) approximately 20 to 40 inches away from a blank wall (a wall without any paintings or objects adorning it).

The practice is to be undertaken whilst facing this wall, in the middle of the mat. With the eyes directed at the wall, the meditating person is less likely to be disturbed by his or her surroundings. This is an important factor, especially at the beginning.

How do I sit?

There are many different ways to sit during the meditation: on a meditation cushion, on a meditation bench, on a stool or a chair.[42] It is important to be in contact with the floor. (The Buddhists say: 'Meditation is not a take-off but a landing.') This is why the cushion or the bench should, if possible, be chosen instead of a chair. When sitting on a stool or a chair, the feet ought to be placed flat on the floor or mat (without shoes). The hands can either rest on the thighs or be folded on the lap. Using the bench or the cushion, the knees (and calves) are to be in contact with the floor.

Sitting needs to be comfortable enough to maintain the posture, without adjusting it, for the whole meditation (at the beginning for a short period of time, e.g. 15–20 minutes, and later on for a longer period of time, 30–60 minutes). There is no reason to attempt positions that cause pain or make your leg or foot fall asleep. What is important, along with maintaining contact with the floor, is holding the upper body upright so that you are able to breathe freely. The head is held straight; the eyes remain – in accordance with Zazen tradition – half open, the gaze slightly lowered and directed at the wall. However, many traditions practise sitting meditation with closed eyes.

How do I meditate?

During the meditation, our mind should strive for a state of *content-free* wakefulness. This does not necessarily mean that one merely passively thinks of nothing in particular. For when we observe ourselves when thinking of nothing, we notice that we never truly think of nothing but rather let our thoughts roam freely, allowing them to come and go spontaneously. Which thoughts thereby enter our consciousness is primarily determined by our emotions – conscious or unconscious. The thoughts that arise within us as words or images in turn affect the emotions, for nearly every thought is connected with a specific emotion. There is a continuous emergence of content in the shape of thoughts and emotions.

Yet, even when we actively attempt to attain the content-free state of mind, we notice that we are dealing with a very difficult task indeed. We are able to concentrate on *something*, we are able to focus our thoughts on *something* and fade out everything else, for instance, when working out a difficult arithmetical problem in our head, or when reciting a text from memory. It is much more difficult to focus on *nothing*. For this reason, using breathing as an aid is recommended. We observe our breathing: Our mind is focused on it and follows the flow of breathing in and breathing out. It is important that we do not seek to manipulate our breathing but go along with it just as it is.

Another aid to achieving the necessary concentration is to utter a word with breathing in mind. The word should be chosen with the idea that it will support our mindset during the meditation – a word like *peace*, *silence,* or *love,* for instance. At the same time, we focus our mind on the emptiness in front of and surrounding us – for example, by listening to the silence surrounding us and within us.

At the outset, we will only be able to approach a content-free mind for a very short time. Thoughts and emotions will arise repeatedly. The same is true for people who have been practising meditation for many years – the continuous emergence of thoughts and emotions in our consciousness is a natural characteristic of our human mind.

The practice is not about suppressing the occurrence of thoughts and emotions. What is important is that we do not allow ourselves to be distracted from the meditation by these *disturbances*, which cannot be controlled. We allow all these thoughts and emotions to pass by and remain focused on our breathing (and our chosen word), which ought to lead us to freedom from content. If we become aware of the fact that a thought is stuck to our consciousness and diverts our attention to its content, we embrace – without judging – the thought that has taken up our mind, and calmly but determinedly return to focus on our breathing. To achieve this, we can think the word *thinking*, 'look' at the specific thought *as a thought* and detach ourselves from it – not to identify with it. In the same way, we are able to deal with emerging emotions and physical sensations. Should the same feelings, thoughts or physical sensations repeatedly emerge and hold us captive, we may name (label) them; e.g.: *fear of an exam, neck pain, daily plan, shopping list, furious with daughter, disappointment with employer.*

The goal is to let go – even when object-free meditation is demanding.

Object-free meditation can sometimes be quite demanding, because active wakefulness requires a certain kind of effort. (This is why many people are able to meditate much more easily in the morning after a night's rest, than in the evening when they are tired.)

Object-free meditation is not practised by merely idly *sitting there*. It is a wakeful *thinking* of nothing or – as mentioned earlier – focusing on breathing or a word carried by the breath: *thinking* in the sense of an active concentration or awareness of the mind.

No extreme efforts to keep the mind free from thoughts should be attempted, however. Attentiveness and perseverance are very important. Yet, the goal is not to desperately cling to the breathing and the accompanying word. Thoughts and emotions are part of us. Object-free meditation is not about suppressing them. It instead is about letting them go, to focus our mind on the space *behind* or *between* the thoughts, feelings, physical sensations and sensory perceptions.

If the mediating person realises that they have been distracted, they should calmly and kindly – time and again anew – direct their attention to the breathing and the chosen word. This attention is not solely with the mind. Our body too is part of the meditation, everything is present, everything ought to be just there – complete alertness but not by means of a strenuous effort. The goal of the practice is to let go of all thoughts and emotions without exertion. This goal is not necessarily reached faster by those who are better at concentrating on the exercise of object-free meditation. The goal is reached when it is reached. *It* happens. The self has no control over it.[43]

Which activities are appropriate for accompanying and supporting object-free meditation?

Especially at the beginning, it can be very helpful to attend meditation classes where, over a couple of days, Zen or Contemplation[44] is practised with others and under the guidance of an experienced person. The author recommends two addresses based on his own experience.[45]

One possible way to support the daily practice is to attend group meditation sessions regularly. Every larger city offers the possibility to attend numerous meditation groups that meet on a weekly basis for one to two hours for mutual meditating. As an additional advantage, experiences can also be exchanged at these meetings.

It can be of help on the path of object-free meditation to read an appropriate text before or after the meditation. A vast array of books are available that could suitably accompany or guide someone on the spiritual path. Deciding which book to choose when commencing the journey is not always easy, so here are some suggestions. They are intended as a starting point for the meditating person to find support in, before coming across the text most suited to him or her specifically.

For those practising meditation as a way to increase self-awareness, the book *Freedom From the Known* by Jiddu Krishnamurti is a suitable one to accompany this process.[46] Another appropriate text is

'Coming to Our Senses' by Jon Kabat-Zinn, which is independent of religious teaching or tradition.[47] Kabat-Zinn is the founder of MBSR (Mindfulness Based Stress Reduction) – an application of mindfulness practice as a therapeutic tool in medicine.

If object-free meditation is practised in the context of the Christian tradition (Christian mysticism), then the texts composed by Tauler and Meister Eckhart can serve very well.[48] Another classic work that can be recommended in this context is *The Cloud of Unknowing.*[49] There are also books written by contemporary mystics, including *Search for the Meaning of Life*[50] by Willigis Jäger or *Into the Silent Land* by Martin Laird[51].

For people who would like to practise object-free meditation within the Buddhist tradition, the books by Charlotte Joko Beck (Zen Buddhism) and J. Kornfield (*classic* Buddhism) are recommended.[52]

Experience shows that reading on a regular basis (e.g. reading a chapter of a chosen book twice a week after an extended sitting meditation) bears the best fruit. It is further recommended to read the selected book from beginning to end, not merely some chosen chapters. Ideally, work through the book in this manner two to four times. Repeated readings and extended meditation help us to get a much better grasp of some texts.

Shorter texts are suitable for meditation groups, to be read out loud either at the beginning or between two rounds of meditation.

'Stay with your own self!'

This phrase from sermon number 73 by Johannes Tauler is cited in order to emphasise that the experience of the practice of object-free meditation is different for every person and can only be individually gained – for myself and with myself. There are many texts and courses available that prove to be important entry points and should initially be seen as essential for most people. However, the path can only be walked by myself alone: *meditating once or twice daily.* At the beginning for 15 to 30 minutes, later on extended to 45 to 60 minutes.

Everyone that practises this will live to see the fruit – a direct experience of perfect freedom, the unconditional acceptance and love. An experience that no human can provide me with – which I cannot bring about myself. An experience that I may receive as a gift by practising object-free meditation.

As stated in the previous paragraph, it is also expedient and important to read about and to listen to what others have experienced. But for all that, such texts and accounts can never replace the individual practice of regular meditation. Of utmost importance is to persevere. Not how I am sitting, or at what hour of the day I meditate, nor what I am reading or what I am feeling whilst meditating is most important, but rather that I stay with the path I have chosen. Only by persevering can this newfound reality merge with my everyday life. I will notice more clearly and often, even during my daily routine, how everything is permeated with and contained in love.

FOUR POSSIBLE PERSPECTIVES

The following chapters present the reader with four possible perspectives, which describe the path of object-free meditation. They can be of help in getting started with regular practice.

The *first* of the four perspectives is that of a human being who gets to know his or her self by means of regular practice. The mantra guiding this person is: *Know thyself / Know yourself.*

The *second* perspective describes the path from the point of view of a human being in search for *meaning.*

The *third* perspective conforms to the original tradition within which object-free meditation has been practised. It is the perspective of a religious human being. The Christian teachings of the New Testament provide its basis. It might as well be any other religion. The Christian tradition has been chosen, because it is the most prevalent and widespread tradition in the western culture in which we live.

The final of these four texts describes the practice of object-free meditation as a path of trust or faith. There, I have to trust in other people's account of the path in order for me to set forth on it. This last perspective poses the question of what it means and what reasons can be given in favour of or against this faith. It additionally shows that the faith I place in myself – in what I am as a human being during my existence on this earth – increases during this journey. Very much like the first, the final perspective focuses on self-knowledge – on the realisation of who I am deep within myself.

The knowing or realisation of my own nature – the essence of what I am as a human being – constitutes an important part of the path, regardless of which perspective the meditating person is guided by. The ideological frame can be different depending on the context: During object-free meditation, the Christian sits in front of God, the atheist and the Zen Buddhist sit in front of the emptiness, the philosopher perhaps in front of the *all-encompassing* that he is not able to grasp with his mind.[54] Meanwhile, all of them are sitting in front of themselves and by themselves. This is the reason why the path of object-free meditation always represents a process of self-awareness. It is a path leading to the self, in the philosophical as well as the psychological sense. This is similar, perhaps, to a mountain that different wanderers climb with different goals. One may want to see the top of the mountain, another hopes to find the sun above the mist in the valley, the third would like to be able to view the entire valley he lives in from the top, yet another to get to know the landscape that lies on the other side of the giant hill. All of them, though, walk the same trail. On their way, they all encounter the same obstacles, menaces, perils, and plants and animals.

Why are four perspectives being presented and not just one – *the* one? This is because every concept around object-free meditation captures only a partial aspect of the processes that take place within the meditating individual. The meditation practice, not any theory, is the vital component of this path. Only in practising, only with the individual human being – the woman or the man – who walks this path, does *the whole* emerge – only then does *the whole* come into existence.

In addition, presenting several perspectives shows, by means of these different examples, that the path of object-free meditation is independent of concepts and teachings.

On the other hand, all of the four concepts described here are valid. They all lead to the same place. However, they become invalid – become untrue – when they are turned into a singularly accepted dogma or ideology. A dogma or ideology that envisions itself as the sole valid teaching, forces what remains intangible to the reason into a prison of dualistic logic. The parable of the blind men who wanted to know what an elephant looks like illustrates the problem.[55] The different descriptions of their perceptions, when they approached the phenomenon of the elephant by means of touch, were all true, not false. Nevertheless all the blind men were wrong, because each insisted that his own description was the only truthful one.

Everyone has to decide for him or herself which of the four concepts is most suited to that person. A devout Christian will choose the third perspective. An atheist will perhaps choose the first one, an agnostic the second. Today, many people in the western culture walk the path of object-free meditation in accordance with Zen or another Buddhist school. The classic Buddhist perspective is clearly described – in a comprehensible manner for us western people – in the recent book by the Dalai Lama, *A Profound Mind. Cultivating Wisdom in Everyday Life.*

Unlike the first part of this book, this second part is not meant to be read thoroughly as a whole. It is rather meant as a guide to regular practice. On a first reading, it might even be better not to read all four descriptions of the path of meditation in succession. The first chapter, *Know Yourself,* and the last, *The Path of Trust,* describe the path most extensively.

Do we need a perspective? Are not patience and perseverance with regular practice more important than a specific concept? Is it not better to just practise?

The answer to those questions is both yes and no. Having reached the point of awakening with regards to the deeper meaning and the experiencing of all-encompassing love, the path that led us there becomes irrelevant. Nevertheless, on the path of daily object-free meditation practice, difficult phases might be encountered, where the concept that guides us allows us to summon the strength and courage to stay on the path.

In this respect, people who practise object-free meditation within a religious tradition benefit from being able to draw on a wealth of experience from many people who have walked that path within that tradition before them. They find devotion to an *idol* (Krishna, Buddha, Jesus, God) to be of great assistance. In Bhagavad Gita, one of the oldest scriptures describing the path, Krishna says: *'Greater is the travail of those whose mind is fixed on the Unmanifest; for it is hard for embodied mortals to gain the Unmanifest-Goal. But those who casting all their actions on Me, making Me their all in all, worship Me with the meditation of undivided devotion; of such, whose thoughts are centred on Me, O Partha, I become ere long the Deliverer.'* [56]

According to this citation from Bhagavad Gita, the path of object-free meditation guided by a non-religious concept (like one of the concepts described in the next 3 chapters) is more difficult. There is no support from a personalised guiding figure. Today, however, it represents the only way for many people who have been socialised in the western culture – who have been taught to view the rational mind as the highest authority and for whom religious concepts are not accessible.

On the other hand, the physical personification even of a religious figure must be abandoned on the way to the unnamed – and the unnamed is where the answer is to be found. The concept merely provides support – like a ladder to reach the top, or a raft to reach the shore. The following tale, which, according to tradition, Buddha relayed to his disciples, illustrates this:

'Monks, I will teach you the parable of the raft – for getting across, not for retaining. It is like a man who going on a journey sees a great stretch of water, the near bank with dangers and fears, the farther bank secure and without fears, but there is neither a boat for crossing over, nor a bridge across. It occurs to him that to cross over from the perils of this bank to the security of the farther bank, he should fashion a raft out of sticks and branches and depending on the raft, cross over to safety. When he has done this it occurs to him that the raft has been very useful and he wonders if he ought to take it with him on his head or shoulders. What do you think, monks? That the man is doing what should be done to the raft? What should that man do, monks? When he has crossed over to the beyond he must leave the raft and proceed on his journey. Monks, a man doing this would be doing what should be done to the raft.

In this way I have taught you Dharma, like the parable of the raft, for getting across, not for retaining. You, monks, by understanding the parable of the raft, must not cling to right states of mind and, all the more, to wrong states of mind.' [57]

1. KNOW YOURSELF

Object-free meditation as a path leading to oneself

'*Know thyself.*' Many great philosophers, artists and spiritual teachers have put forth this phrase as an axiom for life or the essence of their teachings.[58] This is not surprising when we realise that awareness of the self – the ability and desire to gain knowledge about oneself – is quite likely the most important attribute that turns man into a human being. The more I know myself, the more I become human, the more I become what I was born into this world for and now exist as, regardless of how this existence of man, as he is today, came into being – by means of evolution in nature, through a higher principle like God, or by *pure chance.* The more self-aware I am, the more human I am.

Even if I adopt the viewpoint of a solely rationally thinking person, with little interest in philosophy or spirituality, I have to reach this conclusion in consequence of the considerations above. Self-awareness – gaining knowledge of the self – is an ability and trait unique to Homo sapiens.[59] It might therefore be considered one of the most important purposes of every woman and every man during their existence on this earth. It is a meaningful task that is closely connected with another characteristic specific to human beings: the search for meaning.

For the answer to fundamental questions – and these include first and foremost the question of the meaning of human existence – man must look within himself. This is why *Know thyself* was engraved on the portal leading to the Oracle of Delphi, to which in ancient times many made pilgrimages, looking for an answer to their fateful questions.[60]

What does it mean to know yourself?

First, we notice that only I myself am capable of directly perceiving my own *self*. Others cannot observe my inmost being – they merely take a more or less accurate guess based on my behaviour. Therefore, I cannot consult other people to come to know myself – as I really am. I can come to know myself, only when I observe myself.

I thus have to attempt to direct my attention to myself, to direct my gaze inward in a meditative and contemplative manner of observation. There, I have to proceed carefully in order to avoid falsifications and distortions. I observe the interior of my mind and focus on what I *fundamentally* am.

Object-free meditation is dwelling upon introspection

Since the question of self-knowledge has been crucial across many different cultures, meditative practices dedicated to introspection have existed for over 2500 years. A basic form of this meditation practice is object-free meditation. [61] There, we stay in a state of wide wakefulness and interested attentiveness, in the course of which no object – external (e.g. objects or sounds) or internal (e.g. thoughts, feelings or physical sensations) – is focused on. Through regular practice – as described in the chapter *Practising Object-free Meditation* – the meditating subjects acquire the ability to observe their own thoughts, feelings and physical sensations without being distracted by their observations. They also realise, whilst doing so, that while these activities of their mind and body may be a part of them – a part of the person they live as – these thoughts, feelings and physical sensations nevertheless do not constitute their real *self*. They realise that they are not identical to the activities of their mind and body.

This insight, reached during the practice of object-free meditation, is of great importance with regards to the challenge of knowing *yourself*. For this realisation implies that I – my self – am more than my thoughts, more than my feelings and more than my physical sensations. Behind all these activities of our mind resides an observer who is able to perceive them. If it thus says *know yourself*, then the focus must be directed at this observer. There, we become aware that we are able to observe *that we observe* our thoughts, feelings and physical sensations. This means, however, that we are *more* than this observer because we are capable of observing him.[62] This notion of *more* – one could also call it the observer of the observer – cannot be discerned by us because it coincides with the sensation of our *I* or *self* – with the immediate momentary experience.[63]

This direct experience – which we often relate to as the *self* – eludes our observation, because every attempt to observe it always comes to an end with an observer (the observer of the observer etc.): with our *self* that withdraws from observation. For observation by me to take place, I have to observe. I am then not the thing that is being observed but the one who is observing. I cannot observe myself as what I *truly and wholly* am behind all my thoughts, images, feelings, perceptions, fantasies. This however entails that I am not capable of *truly and wholly* knowing myself. (If I am not able to observe myself.)

In this context, object-free meditation is to be regarded as the attempt to linger over this moment that is nearest to this direct observation. That is to say, during the meditation we focus the observer (that which we perceive as our mind or our consciousness – not the observer of the observer, for we cannot control him or her) on the space *between* or *behind* the thoughts and feelings. We focus on the emptiness where they reside.

Not only beginners but also people with many years of experience in meditation have difficulty dwelling with their mind on this emptiness. Therefore, we use breathing as an aid and focus the observer – our mind – on breathing. Whoever has attempted this knows that one is time and again distracted by thoughts, feelings, physical sensations or sensory perceptions. Thus, it is important to guide the observer back in the direction of our focus in order to stay with ourselves.

In this respect, the exercise of object-free meditation can be seen as perseverance with regards to our self-observation. We always return to what we ultimately are, if we leave aside all our feelings, thoughts, perceptions and pretences. As already mentioned, direct observation of my *self* (meaning the *observer of the observer*) is impossible. During the object-free meditation, I remain in the spot that is located closest to this direct observation of my *self*.

The process of self-knowledge is painful

This dwelling on self-observation is not just demanding from a *technical* point of view. Everyone who has practised it over a period of time knows how difficult, tiring and aggravating it can be to repeatedly return the observer to the focus of the meditation. However, it also represents a process of self-knowledge in the psychological and psychotherapeutic sense. The daily routine of practising object-free meditation leads to being aware of ourselves – with all our characteristics – with much more clarity and less distortion than is possible in everyday life.

This interior view furthermore allows us to access aspects of ourselves that had previously been unknown to us. For we are confronted with the fact that many – if not all – of the attributes that we condemn, despise or even detest in other people, are part of ourselves as well. Some schools of psychotherapy describe this as dealing with the shadow; with the aim to eventually integrate this shadow as a part of the *self*.[64]

This process can be demanding and lead to anxiety and self-doubt. It can also awaken memories of psychological damage, experienced during our lifetime, especially in our early childhood. In addition, we come to realise that many beliefs about our inner life that we had regarded as of vital importance can no longer be regarded as unshakable truths – that even our *self* with all our attributes and values, which we had up until then experienced as a stable construct, entails great insecurity and instability.

The path to self-awareness by means of object-free meditation can thus be difficult and painful. With regular practice, however, we also gain more psychological stability and experience a broadening of the horizon of our mind – which enriches us with unforeseen experiences leading to the perception of clarity and joy. Because of the strength that is won from the practice of object-free meditation, it is very important to continue with regular daily practice and to hold on to it. Continuing regular meditation is the only way out of this dark place of unease and despair.

If the regular practice is continued – despite the burdensome experiences – then the object-free meditation ultimately leads to a deeper understanding of our consciousness. The longer we stay with the self-observations, the more clearly we experience the fact that our consciousness – which is located *behind* the feelings, physical and sensory sensations and thoughts – is empty. This empty stage is the space of awareness where the actions of our mind – which manifest as thoughts, images and feelings – take place.

There can even be moments during this process when our *self* – the observer of the observer – appears insubstantial and empty. The encounter with our shadow – meaning the confrontation with the fact that we ourselves carry many undesirable and atrocious attributes within us – connected with this premonition of the possibility that even our own *self* can be experienced as nothingness, can trigger anxieties: the anxiety about losing the *self* and the anxiety, in light of our helplessness, in the face of the shadow within us.

The gift of the experience of the true self

We are only able to conquer these difficulties if we continue to meditate regularly. Especially during this phase, it is important to hang on to the practice – to meet the point of stillness of our mind on a daily basis and to stay with the emptiness of the moment time and again. With the regular practice, the meditating person is ultimately presented with the experience of directly realising the *true self*: he or she thereby experiences something that is *above* the observer of the observer, something that is more than the emptiness, more than the *self* – the dualism between the observer and the observed is suspended. The meditating individual does not distinguish him- or herself from the emptiness within which he or she resides; he or she is the emptiness – which entails everything and from which everything emerges – the individual himself or herself is the stillness that allows love, joy, clarity and the feeling of a deeper meaning to blossom – and this stillness is the individual. The feeling of the self *dissolves* in pure awareness.

We know that this experience takes place, from the accounts of many people who have experienced it and continue to today.[65] How exactly it takes place ultimately remains hidden from the person experiencing it. Logically speaking, the direct realisation of the *self,* as described above – complete, with everything that belongs to me, just as I am – represents a contradiction: I cannot observe myself without some part of my conscious *self* observing too (being the observer and not the observed) and thus remaining hidden from observation. Should this happen, despite all odds, it must happen in a dimension in which the dualism between the observed and the observer is suspended – a dimension beyond thought, beyond the mind.

Not merely by this logical contradiction, but also due to the quality of the experience, the meditating person knows that he or she is encountering a reality that cannot be perceived with reason – a new reality, a reality beyond the reason and beyond the thoughts or feelings, in the spiritual dimension. This reality represents the experience of my true being – my intrinsic, essential being.

This experience allows the meditating person to witness a deeper meaning with regards to their own existence and the existence of all beings. It releases unprecedented pleasure, clarity, freedom and love. The process of self-knowledge, accomplished by regularly practising object-free meditation, leads to an encounter with values that belong to a new reality, to another dimension. The object-free meditation – even when detached from any kind of religious theory or tradition – thus represents a spiritual path.[66]

If and when this experience is being made, it remains hidden from the meditating person. Once it happens, it is a gift. I myself cannot contribute anything to it. I can merely stay with the regular practice. Since the things it deals with lie beyond reason, we are not capable of conceiving them. Imaginations and expectations rather interfere with and keep us away from this experience.

Love as the basic state of human awareness

How does our mind's state of emptiness during object-free meditation lead to this gift of love and joy?

We know that this does happen from the accounts of many who have experienced it. We know that they were able to make this experience after having remained within the stillness for a long period of time, often – although far from always – during the meditation, whilst staying at a place that knows no cravings – where there is stillness and emptiness with regards to feelings and desires. The gift of the experience of love springs from this emptiness. It is a gift as such, because we do not desire anything within this stillness, we do not pursue any goals to be reached – not even in the form of any kind of extraordinary experiences. Whatever happens is perceived as a gift. It is simply there. Based on these experiences, love can be understood as the original condition of the human disposition.[67] Once desires and emotions fall silent, a space is liberated that overflows with love. This is why Krishnamurti says: *'There is no silence without love.'*[68]

The experience of the stillness of the moment – the emptiness, the now – also represents the experience of my true being, my actual *self*. Once everything falls silent, only the consciousness remains – the consciousness that exists when I am free from all external influences. The experience of my true *self* leads to joy. At the same time, it is the experience of the true *you*. I experience not only what I am but also what *you* are. There is no distinction made. *I* as anxiety, *I* as separation, *you* as anxiety, *you* as separation – this is perceived as a partial aspect of the existence on this earth, but not as the being that I live as and that you live as. It is the awareness of the fact that the source of being – what remains if I abandon everything – and thus also the reason for my existence is good. Through this experience, I become aware that the very source of the world – within which I exist as a human being – is good. I, as a human being, feel sheltered in unconditional and timeless love and benevolence.

A long journey, a never completed mission in life

Usually, the way leading to this experience is long. On this journey, time is measured not in weeks or months, but in years. This path leads through the sometimes difficult or very burdensome phases of self-awareness described above, and the search for meaning and stability. However, after having experienced this – once the meditating person has been gifted with this direct experience of the other reality – all hardship is forgotten. The joy, the gratefulness and the love of all and for all, engulf any and all feelings, emotions or thoughts. Women and men who have been given this experience as a gift cannot help but to live out the experienced love – nor can they help but to point out this way of redemption to others.

Until one effectively succeeds in integrating this love into everyday life, more patience and practice are needed.[69] Their encounter with the spiritual dimension does not make people angels or saints. They are, like everybody else on this earth, restricted by the laws of matter and time. They also know – precisely due to their long path of self-awareness – of their weaknesses, of their imperfections and shortcomings as human beings in this material world. However, to them, love and living out this love in everyday life remains the highest principle. They regard this as the first and most important – never completed – task of their lives. A life suffused with a deep meaning, with peace and love.

The path to oneself

(A report of personal experience)

A long winding path, with steps backwards, heights, valleys, cracks and peaks. If I look at myself, look into my inmost being, not stopping to concentrate on what I am – on this unanswerable question – if I retrieve my thoughts every time I notice a deviation to an object or to myself as the subject and continue to look inside, at what is there – right now – within myself, if I attempt to do so once a month, once during a meditation retreat for a week, then more regularly, weekly, daily and then sit there over the course of five years, ten years, for a short period of time at the beginning – fifteen, twenty, thirty minutes – later on for one hour, one and a half hours, two hours, to look into myself, focus on my inmost being, I find emptiness. Absolute concentration on the self finds its conclusion in nothingness, where it dissolves.

From this emptiness emanates – if I manage to endure it, at first merely for a short period of time, later on for longer, for me to be able to observe it – meaning: It, God, Christ, the absolute, the being, the truth, peace... If I stay with it at length and time and again – sometimes I succeed, the next day I find nothing but emptiness – I experience the oneness of It and the sitting, meditating consciousness that I am, which – however – is no longer my self. My being, Hans' being, has dissolved, now there only remains this existence living inside my body. This is the true self, the eternal self, the self that all human beings who walk the same path long enough encounter on their search inwards – a search after knowing the self – in their inmost being. A self independent from my physical existence on this earth, a self that lives equally intensively – and to me as real and effective – in many other people. I take part in this eternal consciousness that bursts Hans' self and perceive it as mercy that I am allowed to experience Its existence and Its workings. A perfect unity sits there, born where I sit, there in this body where my self has died – the self that I sought has dissolved.

This absolute unity has only one purpose: To increase love. Love emanates from the emptiness of my inmost being, love for It, for God, love for all and everything. In order to take on this task, the absolute and eternal returns to the temporality and imperfection of the material world. For only in the material world can love exert its influence, to come to fruition in order to be experienced by others. In the material world, in the temporal world, it is inevitable that mistakes are made. Hans is neither a saint nor a genius. Perfection dies, it is destroyed by this world. Love, however, remains and multiplies. Admittedly, in a very imperfect manner and to a barely noticeable extent, but it nevertheless is a multiplication of love that takes place in this world and time. This is the true existence, the true meaning of Hans' existence. This also is the true self. The self, that depends on eternal love and is careful with every step not to increase suffering.

For my self – my existence, Hans as existence – has caused much harm before coming to this realisation, before this new birth. At his every turn in this world he always craved more, craved something better than the others had. I may never have taken someone's life, but I have hurt many – physically and psychologically. I have disappointed many. Most of all, I have exploited many heartlessly. I bear the blame, Hans bears the blame. I am guilty for something I can never make up for, even if I continue to do good deeds for the rest of my life. This suffering caused by me and by others substantiate love: Great suffering requires great love and the suffering of humankind is endless.

Needless to say, one could hold it against me that this feeling of guilt was misguided, perhaps even a manifestation of a psychopathological condition. Who is responsible for what he is, how he came into this world and the experiences he or she made during early childhood? Experiences which, as we know, have a determining influence on the development of a person. That may be true, but not quite. There is an important difference: I am now aware of the suffering I have caused during my lifetime – and this is a verifiable matter of fact. And in this moment – with the first sight of my behaviour as a cause of suffering from a different plane, the plane of love – I have 'lost my innocence'. I now know of the suffering and I know that I am able to reduce it, if I allow myself to be carried by love. As of this moment I cannot, I must not, act differently. Admittedly, I may be anything but successful in the execution of this important task during my existence on this earth. I repeatedly fall down, misstep and thereby betray the most precious experience of the It that I have received as grace. After every failure, I get up again and sit in front of the emptiness anew, every day. Every day, every hour, a new attempt. Today, as well as tomorrow.

May 2005

2. Man lives on Meaning

Object-free meditation as a rationally substantiated path on the search for the meaning of life

When the literary Nobel laureate and influential philosopher of the 20th century Albert Camus, in his book *The Myth of Sisyphus*, deals with the question of the meaning of life, he encounters an insurmountable gulf between the silence of the world and man who asks the question about the meaning of it all – the question of whether life is worth living. Camus concludes that it stood to reason that life was absurd. Unimpressed by this syllogism, man lives, on a daily basis, from one instant to the other, on meaning.

Meaning is an elementary need and provides us with psychological stability

Our emotional state and our actions are incessantly guided by the assumption that what we are currently doing is – sometimes more, sometimes less – of value. The sense of meaning even provides us with the energy needed to do things that are strenuous and unpleasant. Meaning gives us pleasure and satisfaction. That is how we experience good days. Every man and every woman, meanwhile, knows moments of emptiness, reluctance, shiftlessness and avolition, which usually originate from the fact that we cannot find any meaning in what we do – meaning that would allow us to devote ourselves to a task with enthusiasm. The feeling of meaninglessness can cause a bad mood, but – lasting for a longer period of time – can also lead to the loss of drive and – finally – depression. A deeply felt meaninglessness leads to suicidal thoughts or intent. The other way around, falling ill with depression usually coincides with a loss of the meaning of life.

The meaning of life represents an elementary requirement to every human being and its absence is a threat to mental health. In line with this, there is a psychotherapeutic school – logotherapy – dedicated to the quest for meaning as its therapeutic target. The name derives from the Greek word for meaning (logos). Viktor Frankl – the founder of this school of therapy – frequently quoted Nietzsche – 'He who has a *Why* to live for can bear almost any *How*' – in describing how important meaning is to contentedness and mental health. One could follow this up with: 'Find the meaning, which is absolute, and you have found the key to an always meaningful, rich and thus happy life.' Absolute (derived from the Latin word *absolutus* 'freed, unrestricted') means independent from all influences. Be it difficult interior conditions like self-doubt, loss of faith, feelings of guilt, or psychological or physical pain caused by external events such as severe losses, incurable or disabling medical conditions, disappointments or being treated with contempt by an important person.

Meaning, the feeling of pursuing a desirable aspiration, gives us security. More often than we are aware of, we do not rely on *what we are or think we are* in everyday life, but on short term and momentary aspirations. Towards the close of a day for instance, I look forward to dinner when I am at work – because I am hungry and tired – or I quickly do the dishes (for they have to be taken care of) in order to be able to sit down at the table again and peacefully drink some wine. [70] There, the aim is to satisfy needs, desires and lust. When getting dressed in the morning I make it my aim to be able to go to work. I am already thinking of the tasks I need to take care of in the office. The driving force behind it is ambition. Ambition and the desire for appreciation are important generators of meaning. Our self-esteem heavily relies on appreciation from other people, as well as from our own interior, judgemental authority – what Sigmund Freud termed the *superego*. In order to receive appreciation, we are prepared to accomplish great things, be it by helping and serving or by power and money – the latter commonly serving as a substitute for an absent sense of self-worth. When we ask the question as to why appreciation is so immensely important and desirable to us, we have to notice that the desire for love – the longing to be fully accepted and adopted – plays an important part.

From a rational point of view, there is no meaning

Goals that create meaning have the fact in common that they are not located in the present – where we instantly find ourselves – but in a more or less distant future. The sense of meaning drawn from them is, as a consequence, everything but independent from external and internal events. It happens that we miss our targets – whether that is our fault or not – which can lead to disappointment. It may also be true that I am not even in the position to be able to attain a target due to a psychological or physical illness, or due to the state of the economy or other unfavourable external circumstances. Rather than creating meaning, unachieved targets create a feeling of meaninglessness.

Since meaning derived from goals is set in the future, concerns naturally arise that we will not be able to achieve the specified goal. In consequence of these fears, we begin to protect ourselves from every possible event that could possibly jeopardise the reaching of the aim. This leads to worries and grief instead of pleasure and confidence.

But even if I manage to accomplish a goal – and quite often simply because it has been accomplished – it loses its meaningful effect. This leads to new and greater goals being sought after and striven for over and over again: more power, more money, becoming an even better person, and so forth. It happens quite often that man – on his way up this ladder to greater achievements – suddenly changes his mind and asks himself what is the meaning of all these aspirations. If he is sufficiently honest with himself, he will reach the place that Camus has described in *'The Myth of Sisyphus'*: the feeling of meaninglessness and the absurdity of life.[71]

Other keen thinkers have also arrived at this conclusion that human existence – when looked at rationally – is absurd and meaningless: Solomon, Buddha, Comenius, Kierkegaard, Schopenhauer, Kafka, Heidegger and so on. The author of the Book of Ecclesiastes in the Old Testament phrases this idea in a straightforward and unambiguous way: 'So I hated life, because what is done under the sun was grievous to me, for all is vanity and striving after wind.'

Search for the meaning of life

It is often this profound realisation of the meaninglessness that leads women and men to the search for a higher meaning, be it in philosophy, in religion or in esotericism, which has grown into a large market in these past few years. This search – like the achievements or wishes before – entails a goal to be reached. Sooner or later – if they are serious and honest with themselves – these women and men recognise the fact that a *higher* meaning – that we can rely upon to give us support independently of internal or external events – can only be found within ourselves.

The mystic Angelus Silesius said: 'Travel within thyself! The stone philosophers with wisest arts have vainly sought, cannot be found in foreign parts.'[72] This verse entails a universal truth that is not just spiritually but also rationally comprehensible. *I myself* have to find meaning. If we are to find meaning that yields surety independent from external circumstances and our constantly changing moods then it has to be found in the being itself, in the immediate moment and not in objects or conditions from an uncertain future. Only if man experiences meaning in his immediate simple *being* is it an absolute meaning independent of all external events and internal conditions. If I seek to find absolute meaning, then this is where I have to look for it – within myself.

Everyone who begins their search today can count himself or herself lucky, because we live in a time that looks back on a long tradition of this search. Ever since the beginning of recorded history, countless people tell of the fact that meaning – absolute meaning, independent of everything and everyone – is to be found at this place: In the present moment, in the simplest act of being.

Object-free meditation is a time-tested path on the search for the meaning of life

Different ways that lead to this place have been described. Object-free meditation offers a tried and tested path that many people have experienced. The nature of this meditation exercise can be deduced, almost directly, from a simple realisation: Man is only able to find the meaning of his existence on this earth with the realisation that life as such – simply being in the present moment – carries a profound meaning.

This realisation leads to the question of how man may find meaning in the act of simply being. Many people do not know the state of simply being. Simply being – to simply be, without physical or mental labour – is judged to be part of the realm of boredom and today's man fears little more in life than boredom. This *fear* of being without pursuit or purpose – without meaning – is probably the most important basis on which the economic system of our consumerist society is built. In order to escape boredom, man is ready to pay nearly any price and is willing to take big risks.

The first step to finding meaning in this emptiness would thus have to be to get to know the condition of being in the first place – being, without having to do anything and without having to occupy the mind with something. Only then is it possible to search for a deeper meaning in this simple act of *just being there*. It is quite probable that these or similar thoughts first led people to try object-free meditation over 2500 years ago.

The women and men who have practised this kind of meditation with dedication and perseverance on a daily basis for years have noticed that remaining in the state of pure being gives meaning. This kind of meditation and its effect was first described in Hinduism and Buddhism. Today, object-free meditation is taught and practised in many religions as the *royal path* to experiencing the spiritual dimension. The exercise (as described in the chapter *Practising Object-free meditation*) is simple and thus accessible to all people without any prior knowledge. Nevertheless, the regular daily practice is not easy, because it leads to the self – to heretofore unknown and unsuspected depths that constitute an important part of the internal psyche of every human being. In addition to that, the way is long; we do not speak of days or weeks, but months and years. It thus requires complete dedication and a lot of courage and strength to stay on this path.

Meaning can only be found in personal, direct experience

All religions and schools that view object-free meditation as the centrepiece of spiritual practice lay stress on the practice itself and not on the theory or the concept behind it. Individual, immediate, personal experience is the only way. The *knowledge* of the spiritual reality cannot be communicated by another person or directly adopted from them. It has to be immediately experienced by everyone on their own.

The different spiritual ways furthermore share an emphasis on the fact that the experiences during object-free meditation can individually differ. Thus, there is no predetermined path by which students of meditation are able to pass from one intermediate objective to the next. Even though the reality to which the practice leads is one and the same, the way in which the path is experienced is not bound to a specifically predefined pattern. The experience of this reality always constitutes something new and personally unique, like how every human being in this world is unique.

The different schools that are based on the practice of object-free meditation also have in common the insight that the spiritual reality – the spiritual dimension – cannot be experienced on the rational plane – by means of our reason. I am admittedly able to understand – based on the illustrations in this text – that I am only capable of finding the meaning of life if I can find meaning in the purest being – in the present moment, just as it is, empty, still, before an internal or external event fills it up. This rational realisation only manages to help me up to the point of the theoretical knowledge. It is not capable of leading me to the experience of the empty moment filled with meaning. At this point, direct experience needs to step in for the mind to comprehend. Only the *experience* of meaning allows me to actually find meaning.

This experience is situated beyond logic, beyond thoughts. It is only possible if man remains with the emptiness of the moment, with the stillness, with the pure presence, free from thoughts and feelings. This is also the reason why the meditating person is asked to focus his or her mind on the breathing and eventually on the emptiness between thoughts and feelings. The thoughts and feelings distract us from this place. Without these emotionally invested thoughts, we moreover experience the moment as being empty and without meaning: as boredom. It is, however, exactly this remaining within the emptiness – the regular practising of meditation – that leads us to the realisation that only within this stillness can true meaning arise – true meaning that is always there, albeit concealed. We arrive at the experience of the deepest meaning, of love, of peace and joy – an experience located beyond thoughts and emotions, an experience that exceeds everything we have up until now witnessed. As a result, emptiness is experienced as abundance, as the source of profound meaning, peace and love.

Our existence is grounded in love

Since our mind invariably asks about the cause of what we perceive, it also poses the question of why man is able to gain access to this experience. The spiritual reality is experienced beyond the capabilities of the rational mind and thus also beyond all concepts that would be able to provide answers to this question. Nevertheless – knowing that the experience lies beyond all concepts – a concept can be a helpful support in everyday life or as communication aid.

All accounts of the profound and direct experience of the spiritual dimension share the experience of an all-encompassing love.[73] It is what gives profound meaning to every moment. This experience happens in the stillness, when everything is silent, when our thoughts, our feelings, our expectations – with which our *self* identifies – fall silent.

Once everything is silent – once we cast off everything we believe ourselves to be as a person – only our true being remains. We could thus venture to say that man is able to have this experience because our existence as human beings *resides* in love. If we are able to conceive of God as an all-encompassing entity,[74] then we realise why it says in the Bible: 'God is love.'[75]

However, the meditating person cannot control or deliberately cause this experience. It is perceived as a gift. *It* happens. Practising object-free meditation is not about actively achieving something, but about staying in the moment, remaining with stillness. Only by doing so can this plane – which gives meaning to every moment – be reached. It cannot be reached by reason or willpower.

Whilst experiencing meaning in purely being, I also notice that meaning is always there and that this reality exceeds my person and time – transcends them. This reality is there, independent of whether I experience it in time or not. This experience, this knowledge based on a direct experience, leads to changes in my everyday life. Generally, these changes are not dramatic. Spectacular changes are not uncommonly overshadowed by the ego, which in those cases also plays the first fiddle in a spectacular manner.

I continue to live everyday life supported by small goals. My attitude, however, radically changes. The experience of the plane of being is overwhelming, to the extent that I even know of this deeper meaning in everyday life. This meaning – embedded in the emptiness, in the simple presence, in *nothing* – creates a foundation that provides me with stability that is independent of events occurring in this space-time and encountered by me. I have not become a better person and most certainly not a saint. Yet still, my being on this earth has profoundly changed because it has acquired a different foundation.

And the path continues: I practise object-free meditation on a daily basis, in order to encounter the emptiness in the stillness of meditation within which I am able to see myself and the world clearly with the gaze of love. Not as a search for meaning. I have reached the destination of this search.

I do, though, continue to doubt and despair time and again. I see, possibly with even more clarity, the gaping absence of meaning in human existence described by Camus from the point of view of the logical mind. I am, though, also aware of the fact that the fall into this bottomless pit ends with the emptiness of the moment, which provides profound stability. The aim of the path is no longer the search, but life – living based on values, perceived in the purest being as a gift, with love leading the way. The more and longer I come into contact with them, the more I am able to live according to them in everyday life and thereby stay connected to them even there.

3. THE PRAYER IN SPIRIT AND TRUTH[81]

Object-free meditation as a spiritual path of Christian mysticism

The Gospel of Jesus

Christianity, as reported in the Gospels of the New Testament, is not an ideology that is supposed to be implemented by means of a revolution or by an organisation – like the church. It is a distinct *message* directed at the individual person. [82]

Nor is it only a moral codex meant to lead to an improvement of our behaviour. The Gospel of John says 'You must be born again' (John 3:7). This means that I am not expected to better myself and thus turn my *self* into something divine – at all times behaving perfectly, absolutely pure and sacred. Christianity is the genesis of a new dimension, the making of a new *life*. Rebirth also means death of the old. This is why Jesus says that whoever shall attempt to save his life, is going to lose it – but whoever loses it, will save it (Luke 9:24). I must not seek to improve my *self* with the desperate aim to improve bad things until a new *self* emerges. It is a radical change: The old must die – the new is born.

Being born anew from the *Spirit* is a process that I cannot manipulate by my will. 'The wind blows where it wishes, and you hear its sound, but you do not know where it comes from or where it goes. So it is with everyone who is born of the Spirit' (John 3:8).

However, an act of will is necessary in order to choose God and acknowledge God as the sole firm point in my life.[83] An unconditional devotion – today we would say a full commitment – is needed. Jesus says: 'If anyone would come after me, let him deny himself and take up his cross and follow me.' (Matthew 16:24).

Once I have made my choice, then the highest – noblest – commandment that I must strive for is: 'Love God.' The second commandment, which emanates from the first, reads: 'Love your neighbour as yourself' (Matthew 22:37–39). The third: 'Love your enemies' (Matthew 5:44).

It is not easy to walk this path. It is an arduous path, full of disappointments. Soon after my decision – to live for God, to love God and to love my neighbour – I realise that I cannot implement this decision in my life. Not even in thoughts. This is the case with every human being. Without an act of the *Spirit of God* – today we would say, without proceeding to the *spiritual* plane – man is not able to walk this path. I cannot advance by well-intentioned will alone.

I find help in prayer. Reading and listening to sermons and exegeses is very important and good. For the *new birth* to take place, however, the *Spirit of God* has to act within me and this is only possible if I turn my attention to God.

In prayer, only I am before God. In a sermon, on the other hand, there is a third person – the minister or teacher – present. I thus cannot be sure if everything I am receiving comes from God. Some preachers and teachers have many followers not because of God but because they fascinate other people with their own personality.

In prayer – alone with God – I experience either God or myself. To be sure it is God and not myself, I have to attempt to be silent, to hold back my mental activities. Only when I am 'poor in spirit' (Matthew 5: 3), meaning once I completely retreat into emptiness, am I able to perceive God. This takes place most effectively during object-free meditation[84] – often called contemplation in the tradition of Christian mysticism.[85] During the object-free meditation my mind is silent.

The *connection to God* cannot take place in our head, with our thoughts. In the Gospel of John, Jesus says: 'God is spirit, and those who worship him must worship in spirit and truth' (John 4:23). Therefore, the prayer to God has to take place on the *spiritual* – and not the intellectual, conceptual or volitional – plane. It has to take place on the plane of the direct experience of the *Spirit*, the absolute that lies beyond thoughts and words. A prerequisite for this experience to take place is *the emptiness of the heart* – laying open the soul's ground during meditation. In the *Sermon on the Mount* Jesus thus says: 'Blessed are the pure in heart, for they shall see God' (Matthew 5:8).

The *connection to God* cannot be exerted with the thoughts or the conscious will, it happens unconsciously – it is not performed by man but has to *happen* to him. This is why Jesus says in the Gospel of John: 'The wind blows where it wishes, and you hear its sound, but you do not know where it comes from or where it goes. So it is with everyone who is born of the Spirit' (John 3: 8).

The start of the meditation, however, needs to be induced by an active, volitionally controllable mental performance. Man has to choose to meditate. This decision and the beginning of prayer therefore have to take place on the conscious plane – that is to say, on another plane than the actual inner prayer: by means of active content-free wakefulness, where our mind is focused on nothing at all or purely on breathing.

This still, content-free presence clears the way (on an unconscious plane) for the *connection with God*. Since the layer of memories, feelings and desires that cover the ground of the heart is very thick, a long time (weeks, months, years) is needed before anyone can experience the absolute peace, the *contact* with the

Eternal. Once it ensues, it is perceived not as an aim that has been reached, but as a gift and grace.

And if I continue to perform this practice long enough, on a daily basis, God will *speak* to me. Differently to each and every one, since it represents an individual connection between God and the person who is praying. However, each individual will feel the love of God, the peace of God.

The object-free meditation described in this book most certainly does not represent the only possibility to directly turn towards God and directly experience the peace of God. According to statements made by teachers and masters, however, it is a reliable way and one that every human being can embark on.

Only once I have experienced the love of God myself, am I able to truly love God – without reservations, without any will, 'with all my heart'. I am so overcome with the love with which God loves me that I cannot but love Him. I thus know that God loves me; I have arrived at the right place. Not because I am something, not because I have done or haven't done something, but simply because I am, because God is too and loves me, because I love God. I am with God, this is the right place for me, God loves me and I love God.

After the meditation, back in everyday life, we realise that we cannot cope with life much better than before. And even if we are much more capable of perceiving the love of God and the presence of God in everyday life, we know that failure is always a possibility – because we carry the 'treasure' we have received from God in 'jars of clay' (II Corinthians 4:7).

I fall down time and again. For days on end, the moments when I perceive God's love – and have the feeling that I love God, and that I love my neighbour as I love myself – can be rare or may not come at all. I fall back to my old *self* over and over. My impuissance drives me to desperation. Whatever can *poor* me do about it?

After a while, I might arrive at the conclusion that I have to give up. I cannot however do this, for I have learned that after having abandoned everything – after having lost everything that seemed to give me security – I have fallen into the arms of God. If I give up, I will again end up with God.

Man should continuously endeavour to live life according to *the righteousness of God*.[86] It is, though, much more important that man knows that the love of God is always and ever present. It is also present in everyday life, even when my *self* is not behaving as it should. God loves me. That is a fact that I am able to sense in an immediate and overwhelming way in many moments, especially during prayer. The fact that God loves me is, however, not just the case in the moments when I immediately sense this.

This too needs to be individually experienced by each and every one and it can once more take a long time until – after the initial direct experience of the love of God during prayer – this grace is received: the certainty that the love of God is there, always there. The certainty that it is not about wanting to be a different *self* – a better person, a better woman, a better man – but about loving God. It is about loving God because He loves me.

Love

From this insight grows a spontaneous and immediate love for one's neighbour. The assurance that God continually loves me – not just during prayer but also in everyday life – that He is present with His love even when I am not thinking of Him – even when I *sin* – makes me realise that God loves other people just the same as He loves me. I realise that other people are equally important to Him as I am. Therefore, I cannot but love others as I love myself, to care about 'my neighbours' as much as I care about myself.

This love stems from God. God loves me; this is also the source of my love. 'In this is love, not that we have loved God but that he loved us' (I John 4:10). With the same love which I experience when I turn to God, I love God, and through God – with God – I love myself and others.

This is the meaning of the two commandments – which Jesus named the two most important ones – and this is why the first commandment must precede the second one: 1. 'You shall love the Lord your God with all your heart and with all your soul and with all your

mind.' 2. 'You shall love your neighbour as yourself'
(Matthew 22:37–39). The first commandment is the
most important; the second commandment allows me
to realise God's love in the here and now, and to
perceive of the state that my love for God is in. 'If
anyone says "I love God," and hates his brother, he is a
liar; for he who does not love his brother whom he has
seen cannot love God whom he has not seen' (I John
4:20).

4. THE PATH OF TRUST

Object-free meditation as a path of trust leading to trust

'In being present we are awake and able to experience love as the deep origin of being.
Louise Reddemann[87]

'(...) our nature (reveals itself) as simultaneously a localized and an infinite expression of wisdom and love.'
Jon Kabat Zinn[88]

'Silence is full of love and compassion.'
Larry Rosenberg[89]

'There is no silence without love.'
Jiddu Krishnamurti[90]

'The flute of the Infinite is played without ceasing, and its sound is love.'
Kabir[91]

'God is love, and whoever abides in love abides in God, and God abides in him.'
The Bible[92]

What do the authors of these texts have in common? There are and have been – ever since the beginning of the history of humankind, at all times and in different cultures – women and men who know that they, at the deepest core of their being, reside in a safe ground. This knowledge does not stem from a specific religious or spiritual dogma, but from their experiences; they have witnessed it. The term many have used to describe this experience is *love*. Love as unconditional acceptance, as a *place* where I[93] know that I am safe. Various texts use different words to describe this experience: freedom, peace, truth or life. It is a quality that gives the human condition a deeper meaning. The experience of absolute trust, of a *foothold* – that is present even in blank despair.

These women and men believe that what they have experienced is also accessible to other people – they believe that the lives of all people are contained, in the deepest core of their being, in love.

Some of them have heralded this *good news* and invited other people to walk a path leading to this experience. This path is a path of trust leading to trust: In order for me to set forth on it, I have to have faith in what these people give account of. Along the way, my faith is strengthened and assured. It ultimately leads to the absolute[94] trust in this primal ground within which I truly reside – a trust that is independent from my ever-changing inner condition and external living conditions.

The initial trust, or faith, that leads to my decision to set forth on this path is often connected to the fact that the message appeals to me. I sense that the citations at the beginning of this chapter resonate with me because something within me knows this love. Or I realise that my life in this world does not provide me with stability and thus seek – perhaps in sheer despair – something that keeps me grounded. A third possibility for the decision to set forth on this path might be the desire for something new, a curiosity or the need to experience as many dimensions of the human existence during my lifetime as possible.

The reason or the motivation for setting forth on this path is less important than the decision to walk on it.

Where does this path lead?

It leads to myself. A place where – independent from external circumstances and inner states – I find stability that cannot be chanced upon outside, with other people, institutions, religious schools or certain conditions in life. A safe ground that I am able to trust in always must be found within myself. Otherwise, it would not be independent from circumstances or other people.

The path commences when I start to place my trust in the accounts of these women and men. They have realised that this place is part of their human condition – part of their existence as a human being in this world. I am a human being. Therefore, what they proclaim means that this place also exists within me. If I place my trust in them, then I believe and have faith in the assertion that my very basis is found in love – in unconditional acceptance.

What does it mean to have faith, to trust?

What does it mean to not have faith, to not trust? In principle, there could be three reasons for not believing in something.

I may have looked into it and established by first-hand experience or by means of information gathered from a reliable source that it is not true. For instance, if I read somewhere that formal Buddhism never actively exerted violence (contrary to, for example, Christian clergy who have supported wars, tortured fellow human beings and had them burnt at the stake), I do not believe it, because it is a historical fact that even in Buddhism, violence – including some gruesome methods of it – was used against other people.[95]

Or, if I am dealing with something that is not verifiable, it follows that I believe in something else which is at odds with the subject of my disbelief. For example, if I hear a Buddhist or Hindu scholar describe a rebirth into this world after death as part of human life, then I might not believe this because I am convinced – owing to the tradition within which I have been brought up, or by virtue of my worldview – that reincarnation does not exist.

Finally, not believing in something may be a result of my experiences with the source of information. If, say, somebody had already promised on four occasions to get me tickets for a Champions League match and never delivered on his promises, I would probably not believe him a fifth time.

To put my trust in someone, or to have faith in something, presupposes that none of the three reasons listed above apply. Firstly, there should be no reason to doubt that these people existed and that the citations at the beginning of this chapter are theirs. These are facts that can be readily verified, especially since some of those people are still alive today.

Secondly, we would have to have no reason whatsoever to think that these people spoke of things they never experienced, that never happened – that they knowingly lied. There is no reason to assume that the accounts are not authentic. They are people who have proven their integrity as well as their closeness to reality and down-to-earthness by the way they conduct their life. In addition, a high degree of self-awareness argues against the assumption that their experience of the primal ground of being was self-deceit or the result of autosuggestion. However, they are also no saints, but people with human foibles and faults. In comparison with other women and men, they stand out for seeing their own flaws and not denying them but acknowledging them as part of human existence.

Therefore, there is no reason not to place faith in the citations listed above.[96] Certainly not concerning the personal experiences. Insofar as these women and men give account of things they have experienced themselves, there is no reason not to believe them.

However, if their accounts imply that this primal ground within which they find themselves was part of the human condition and thus can be experienced by other women and men, then that would be an assertion exceeding their personal experience.

At this point the path begins. Only if I set forth on the path am I able to validate the assertion that it is part of the human condition and that other people – and hence myself – are able to experience it as well. [97] Or the path does not begin. In that case, I decide not to set forth on the path.

There are ample reasons not to set forth on the path

The path requires much time and perseverance. If I decide to set forth on it, then I will *lose* at least half an hour – probably a full hour – of every day. This entails having one hour less at my disposal – one hour less for work, playing, art, enjoyment or thinking about interesting subjects – on a daily basis.

The way is long. If I seek to set forth on it, I have to know that time is not measured in days or weeks, but years.

The path can lead through difficult phases. It is a way to myself. The longer I walk it the better I get to know myself. Within myself I encounter everything I dislike in other people. To endure this, and to stay on the path, can be difficult.

For these three reasons, even some women and men who are in principle inclined towards the path described here, abandon it.[98]

What are the reasons for walking this path?

The path leads, according to the accounts of the women and men who have walked it, to – quite simply – the most important experience of our lives. An experience that allows us to directly perceive the true meaning of our life in this world.

The encounter with this dimension of human existence has been compared to the quest for a treasure – a diamond or a pearl – for which a man is ready to abandon everything. It has been compared to the birth of a child. With the birth of a child, many parents experience a previously unknown joy and bliss that they cannot rationally explain. The birth of a child arouses the intense feeling that life makes sense. This is connected to the fact that, from a biological point of view, the purpose of every living being is the preservation of its species. With the birth of a child, the mother and father fulfil this task. It most certainly does not make their life more comfortable or easier, but gives them deeply felt meaning.

Our existence as human beings, however, cannot simply be narrowed down to the biological dimension. If that were the case, our life span need not be longer than 40 or 50 years. At that point, our children have usually grown up and are able to provide for their own descendants. Similar to how *the biological task* of a human being living on earth entails giving life to new human beings and cherishing them as children, the meaning of my existence as a human being on the spiritual or existential plane – one could say, my *spiritual or existential task* – is to experience love as the primal ground of my being and the being of all people. Love as unconditional acceptance and compassion is the greatest good that man knows.

The path brings me to myself. I am turning into what I am, as a human being, at my deepest core. There, I am able to find absolute stability and answers to the existential questions of the human condition. The aim is not to find a place somewhere with a guru or in a country – where I live in nirvana – but a *place* within myself – the experience of absolute trust in the primal ground where I find myself. If I experience this trust within myself, I also gain trust in myself as a human being living right here and now in the world. One could say, I have now obtained an absolute self-confidence. Absolute, because it does not rely on a concept nor on any abilities but on the immediate experience of what I am at the core.

This *place* is furthermore the origin of ethical and moral values I have got to know by tradition – within which I have grown up. The ethical values cannot be rationally deduced. Karl Popper, a leading philosopher of the 20th century, even said that every rational discussion or action – including those relating to natural sciences – presupposes ethical principles that cannot be grasped by rational reasoning alone.[99] This is why Immanuel Kant speaks – when treating the *practical reason*, the philosophy applicable in practice – of a *categorical imperative*. Something that was handed down to us, which we find within ourselves as human beings. This imperative can be found in one form or another in accounts of important spiritual experiences reaching back more than two thousand years.[100]

In the spiritual dimension,[101] man encounters ethical and moral values in their origin. The Dalai Lama speaks therefore about a *fundamental wellspring of ethics* that all human beings can find in the core of their hearts.[102] During this experience of the primal ground, I come into contact with this dimension and also the origin of ethics and morality. I do not experience them as commandments or prohibitions, but values that I strive to integrate into my life after having had this experience.

What keeps me from absolute trust?

If I had absolute trust in what I am as a human being in my existence in this world, I could also experience the safe ground in myself, the primal ground of the being where I – and all other people – reside. The primal ground is there. That's what Louise Reddemann means when she says '(...) and are able to experience love as the deep origin of being.' That's what Krishnamurti means to say in the citation at the beginning of this chapter, 'There is no silence without love.' Once we are completely with ourselves, in the stillness of the moment, we experience this love. That is what Jesus means when he said: 'Blessed are the pure in heart, for they shall see God.'[103] That is also what Gangaji alludes to with the title of her book: '*The Diamond in Your Pocket.*'[104] That is how she has experienced it. She, nonetheless, had to cover a long journey before finding this diamond.

Why does it take a long journey? What keeps me from having absolute confidence in this primal ground, and ultimately myself? Why do I not have this confidence?

Absolute trust means giving up every pretence, every dishonesty with regards to myself. If I had complete confidence in myself, I would not need to deceive myself. I would be able to see myself in an unbiased way, exactly as I am.

I hardly ever see myself as I am, though. I am everything but unbiased with regards to my own self. Just as I cannot be unbiased with people who are close to me and important to me – for instance, I see my own children differently to the children of my neighbour – I cannot be unbiased toward myself. Much is at stake. It is about my *image*, about how I see myself – what I believe to be myself – about my sense of self-worth.

Every human being has things in life that they know of but regularly and successfully block out. For I do not want to, or cannot, accept that they are part of me. I know, for instance, that I am able to feel not only compassion but also schadenfreude when I learn that my co-worker – with whom I am friends but also in competition – has fallen severely ill. If I look deep into myself, I am able to detect a feeling – if not schadenfreude, then perhaps a pleasant feeling for having gotten rid of the rival – within myself. If I cannot see it, that means that I have either not looked into myself hard enough or that I have been successful in burying or suppressing these emotions.

Owing to my upbringing, I know that emotions such as these are bad, but I want – as every man and woman essentially wants – to be a good human being. I therefore suppress these emotions and refuse to admit them, in order not to be a bad human being. If I continue to suppress these emotions for years on end, then it turns into a pattern – a conditioning largely proceeding unconsciously.

This example might be true for some people and not for others. However, the process illustrated by the example is typical of all human beings: repeatedly suppressing emotions that have been classified as *not good* during their socialisation has turned into an unconscious conditioning.

The example describes a behavioural pattern that mostly takes place unconsciously, but is detectable with deeper insight. Similar patterns, learned in the course of a lifetime, can take place completely consciously and others – where profound suppression took place – remain, even if I look deeper into myself, hidden. Countless patterns such as these, on all three planes of consciousness, (conscious, retrievably unconscious, unconscious) are part of our conditioning as human beings. They have arisen from a combination of our predispositions and from our upbringing and other forms of socialisation.

We could ask ourselves the question why people develop these patterns and guard them even when they create an obstacle to the most important experience we can have during our existence in this world.

First, conditioning arises from the fact that we depend on living with other people in a community. A community can exist only if we learn to not carry out aggressive impulses. Mastering these behavioural patterns can thus be seen as a necessary condition for the existence of human civilisation. At the same time, suppressing the emotions and impulses that are disapproved of by the community makes our lives much easier and more pleasant. I can conceive of myself as a good human being, or at least not as a bad one.

The first step to becoming unbiased with oneself should therefore be: to realise that I am biased. Because I am biased, and aware of this fact deep within, I cannot have unconditional trust in myself. The missing trust *obstructs access* to this primal ground.

To put down the glasses

It is as if we were wearing *rose-coloured glasses* that made the world around us shine more brightly. Imagine there were glasses that would shift your sight to the point where you perceive everything as pleasant – or at least not as bad. These glasses would have a guarantee that lasted a lifetime – meaning you would not need to experience any more unpleasant things for the rest of your life. Would you put these glasses down – assuming that you knew that you were wearing them – in order to see the world and yourself without distortion – just as you are, just as the world is?

If your answer is yes, then truth means more to you than a guarantee of walking through life without unpleasant sentiments; or to put it differently: satisfaction and happiness are not possible for you in life, if you are aware of the fact that they are based on a delusion.

With delusion, without truth, no absolute trust is possible and without absolute trust in myself, there is no circumstantially independent meaning and peace to my existence as a human being. Complete absence of prejudice would mean that I am ready to put down any kind of glasses – rather than perhaps to simply put an additional pair on top.

The Path

The path of trust leading to trust requires putting aside all the many glasses we are wearing. This entails two things: the decision to walk this path and the practice through which we learn to notice the glasses and are able put them aside.

A definite decision is important. Taking off the glasses can be unpleasant and uncomfortable – and the way is generally long. The decision rests upon my trust or faith in what women and men who have walked this path recount. If I place my trust in them, I also place my trust in myself. I have faith in the notion that I am capable of experiencing this primal ground deep within me where I reside as a human being and am safe.

The practice

The exercise with which I am able to learn of my bias – of the *glasses* – can be found in object-free meditation.[105] There are numerous other meditative or non-meditative (for instance, body-related or cognitive and behavioural) techniques that are recommended and taught, but object-free meditation is one of the most reliable and direct practices – the experience of it reaches back more than two thousand years. It is a fundamental form of the meditation that has been practiced in Zen, in Christian contemplation, in the Vipassana-Buddhism, and also in mindfulness-based stress management. Very much as with any kind of practice through which I can learn something, it is important with object-free meditation to practise it regularly – preferably on a daily basis.

By means of regular practice, I build a deep trust in myself. Not in my corporal or intellectual abilities, not in my ethical and moral conduct, but a confidence in myself as I am. Because of the practice, I therefore come closer to myself, to what I am at the core. Figuratively speaking, I thereby put aside the glasses that distort my view and see myself as I am. Only if I see myself without prejudice – without the glasses that colour or demonise – am I able to trust in what I see and trust in what I am as a human being.

In order to put the glasses aside, I have to realise that I am wearing them in the first place. I have to become clearly aware of the fact that I do not see myself, and do not want to see myself, as I am – that I am biased. What are these glasses? They consist of the ideas and imaginations I have about the world and myself.[106] At times they are expressed in my thoughts. Mostly they remain *unspoken*; I am partly or totally oblivious to their existence.

For instance, suppose that whilst I am waiting on the platform for the train, a mother trying to hurry past me with her pram instead ran straight into me, spilling the coffee I was looking forward to drinking on the train, all over my coat. If I suppress the feeling of anger and the thought 'What a cow!' and do not start screaming in exasperation, then underlying this behaviour is the unspoken notion: I am a civilised, perhaps even good human being, who does not know these *primitive* emotions and impulses. In that case, I am seeing myself through the lenses of this notion. One might also call it a kind of hypocrisy towards myself which I am unaware of.

To become aware of the glasses means to realise that I have suppressed my feelings of – *and* refused to believe in my ability to feel – fury or anger and my aggressive impulses. I do not wish to be a human being who has these *primitive* emotions like anger and aggression after having been accidentally run into by a young mother with her pram. I suppress these emotions the second they arise and put on the glasses with which I see myself as a balanced, composed human being who does not know of anger and aggression. Perhaps I suppress these undesirable emotions so swiftly that I am able to claim that they did not occur in me.

We have been taught to control our aggressive impulses by our upbringing and socialisation and it is important that we do have this control. It is a good thing that we do not start screaming and thereby make the day of the already stressed-out mother even more difficult than it undoubtedly already is. However, restraining these aggressive impulses is not what is meant by *the glasses*.

Our upbringing and socialisation have instilled another behavioural pattern in us: If these emotions are provoked in you, then you are a bad person, and a bad person is subsequently rejected. In order to be accepted, I mustn't be *bad*, I mustn't have these feelings – feelings that are not experienced by a civilised, *good* person. This is what our conditioning looks like in western European culture. The suppression of aggressive impulses is necessary for us to not constantly fight with each other and to be able to live together as a community. The fact that our upbringing entails an element of rejection, with regards to aggressive and hurtful behaviour, might perhaps represent a *necessary evil*. It constitutes an important part of our education, without which our civilisation could not possibly be attainable.

It also, however, entails the unwanted side effect that we do not see ourselves as we are. It requires that we suppress our emotions and impulses which would have caused rejection, and thus believe that we are not capable of experiencing them. Otherwise, we wouldn't be the civilised and good people that we are.

This suppression and the glasses that go with it – with which we perceive ourselves and the world around us – result in the fact that we do not place trust in ourselves. We are constantly under the thumb of the mostly unconscious fear that we might lose control. For this reason, we do not trust other people either, because we assume, perhaps justifiably, that they are the same. Because of this universal mistrust, aggression is present in our interpersonal relationships – aggression which might be expressed in a subtle or concealed way but is never less hurtful for all that.

This fear and the lack of trust in myself as a human being can lead to doubts about myself and a lack of self-worth. The glasses I am wearing no longer gloss over anything but actually darken everything. I am worth nothing and capable of nothing. Even this change into negativity depicts a distortion. It arises from a feeling of powerlessness and a fear of not living up to society's and my own requirements and demands. To perceive these glasses means to become aware of the complex and manifold conditionings of human beings in the western European culture of the 21st century.

I can read these explanations and more or less believe them to be true. I can, however, only see the glasses *I* am wearing, once I am ready to put them aside. For, as soon as I see them, I have already put them aside and no longer see the world through them. I am only able to realise that I have seen myself and the world through these glasses after having taken them off. The way they distort our vision differs from person to person. There are also differences with regards to how strongly the various negatively connoted impulses and emotions exist within a woman or a man and to which degree they are acted out or suppressed, respectively. [107]

In order to become aware of the glasses and to put them aside – to see myself as I am – I must be able to clearly perceive my thoughts, emotions and motives. Thoughts and emotions are so closely linked that we often cannot differentiate them. Nearly every thought is accompanied by an emotion; emotions create new thoughts in turn.

Throughout the day, countless thoughts and emotions reach our mind. Between twenty and sixty thousand thoughts come and go through the day – and most of them were already there the day before. We barely notice this constant circulation of thoughts and emotions during our everyday life. The practice of object-free meditation helps us to notice and observe them. I normally do not notice my thoughts and emotions because I *am* them: I identify with what I think and feel – and unconsciously am moving in a circle alongside them.

I can only clearly perceive my thoughts and emotions once my mind is still – once it is not constantly moving with the thoughts. We cannot wilfully calm our mind on command, just like we cannot tell ourselves to go to sleep. Everybody who has – perhaps during meditation – attempted to, knows this. I cannot control my thoughts either. They come and go without me being able to stop or do away with them.

However, experience shows that we achieve stillness within when we focus on, and our minds remain with, an object. This object may be a picture, a word or breathing. We focus our attention on this object and return to it every time we realise that we have been distracted by external or internal stimuli. This experience is as old as meditation. It led to mindfulness of breathing – a practice that has stood the test as a basic form of meditation for millennia and constitutes a vital component of object-free meditation.

Everyone can, even today, directly experience its effect. Different people will take a different amount of practice until their mind calms down and they are able to experience this inner stillness. Some may experience it already after a couple of days – or even during their first meditation – and some may need several weeks or months. However, with sufficient practice everyone is able to experience this inner stillness where our mind comes to rest.

During the exercise of mindfulness we bring our mind to rest and look inward, look at our own being. What do we see? We see, as already mentioned, thoughts and emotions that constantly arise. Once our mind is still, we are able to see them much more clearly. We are thus able to discern them as pleasant or unpleasant, as memories concerned with the past or as plans for the future. Once we observe them during a meditation over a longer period of time, we realise that we are not these thoughts.

Observing my thoughts, emotions and impulses leads to an increase of self-knowledge. I am able to see what kind of mundane and *primitive* thoughts are part of me. On the other hand, the trust in myself increases too. This act of perceiving my own emotions and thoughts leads to the awareness that I am more than these thoughts and emotions with which I identify. I become aware of the space *behind* these thoughts and emotions, a room where they are kept. It is a *space of stillness* where I am kept too.

Daily meditation also induces a general strengthening of our mental stability. This is one of the reasons why meditation is used in psychotherapy.[108] Both the increase of trust and the general strengthening of our psyche are processes that are not consciously perceived by the meditating person. We only notice the result. However, our conscious trust in the way increases as well: I have set forth on the path without having been aware of the glasses that have distorted the view of myself and the world. I am now aware of them; the way leads to a clearer view of all things that are of importance to me in life.

The increase of mental strength and trust are important. They sustain the meditating person and give him or her the courage to stay on the path even during difficult phases.

Why can this path occasionally lead through difficult phases?

In the course of meditation, and also in everyday life due to the practice of meditation, many things become clear to me – things that I would not have noticed before. I become much more aware of my thoughts and intentions and realise that – if I am being honest – there are hardly any negative features that I deplore in other people that could not – at least as a seed – be found within me as well. Be it envy, hatred, malevolence, selfishness, vanity, sexual drives, violent visions or hunger for power. Psychotherapy speaks of an encounter with one's own shadow[109] – with the parts of my personality that I reject and therefore am mostly unaware of.

I realise too that the surety I have found in the things I have placed my trust in is unreliable and always temporary – be it plans for education or a profession; be it pleasure, work, prosperity, performance, benefaction or power. This realisation is painful and can lead to insecurity or desperation. It is as if the path to trust had to lead through a temporary loss of trust.

During these phases, it is especially important to continue to practice meditation. The desperation and the emptiness I encounter – when I am able to clearly see the different parts of my person and the reality of my existence as a human being – show the place where I am kept and experience an unconditional acceptance independent of my attributes. A look full of love; I turn towards myself – with everything I am – lovingly. Jon Kabat-Zinn writes about mindfulness meditation in the book cited at the beginning of this chapter: 'It is an act that (...) is ultimately one of pure love (...).'[110]

However, this *look* is not something I can reach volitionally. On the contrary, my self needs to step back in order for this place to become visible. The more I long for it, the harder it is to see. The experience of this place is gained once I have completely surrendered myself. Only when I abandon all pretences and concepts of who I am, which provide me with a feeling of security and out of which the image of my self is made, can I witness something that is more than my *self*, something that is bigger than what I am. At this place, I need not comprehend, grasp or keep hold of anything with my *self*. This is where my being is kept in love and absolutely safe.

Viewed in this light, difficult phases are a *positive* thing because they lead to the place of absolute trust. They can also be perceived as a *positive* thing from a purely psychological point of view. These negatively connoted features have always been present; the only difference is that I am now aware of them. There is thus no reason why I should condemn myself. I haven't become *worse* simply because I now see myself clearly. On the contrary, I am now able to see these parts of me, which is why they become less effective – they have less control over me.

These features are furthermore part of the human condition. They originated either in innate drives and instincts or in our conditioning brought about by our upbringing and socialisation as human beings in the present-day western civilisation. Therefore, I do not need to condemn myself, should I spot them within me. I can accept them as a part of me, as something that is part of me as a human being.

I realise that this unconditional acceptance applies to me as I am – including these features that I dared not face for such a long time. Thus, I am able to confidently gaze inward, free from the fear of encountering new things. (For I encounter new emotions, desires and drives every day, there is an inexhaustible supply; I will never have encountered them all.) I can look deeply within my innermost being, where I am able – in trusting – to find absolute trust. The place where I find myself kept in an all-encompassing love.

The path is long

This path is not one where results and great successes can be attained within a few days or weeks. The way to the experience of the primal trust, the all-encompassing love, of knowing that I am accepted as I am, is long. It can be cumbersome but is never boring. It leads through difficult phases, described above, but also sustains us on a daily basis – it provides us with strength gathered from the direct encounter with our self. It strengthens my trust and helps me to get through difficult times or crises – which I go through during my life – without getting lost in desperation. The more clearly I see myself – exactly the way I am – the firmer the ground on which I stand becomes, the ground in which I am able to trust. This is so not just during the meditation but also and above all in everyday life.

Just words

This text has attempted to describe a way on which a person is able to find absolute *foothold* – provided he or she sets forth on it with trust and perseverance. The experiences and the psychological processes described here are meant as examples; they describe what many people – who have walked this path or are still walking it – have reported. However, the way is different for every individual. The individual experiences are as unique as the lives of every single human being. The descriptions should therefore not be read as a *guide* to what a person ought to experience but as an example that perhaps motivates the reader to set forth on this path. The way itself is always and ever individual and unique.

The text speaks time and time again of the place where the path ends. This place alone is something that cannot be put into words. The experience of this place lies beyond thoughts and emotions and thus also beyond the possibility to appropriately describe it by means of words. A word or concept turns it into an object – an object that we believe in can be grasped with our reason. When this happens, it is turned into a lifeless word and cannot provide a solid and safe ground.

Man cannot arrive at knowing this place by means of words or images but solely by setting forth on this path ourselves.

PART III:
THE PATH CONTINUES

INCORPORATING SPIRITUAL VALUES INTO EVERYDAY LIFE

The aim of all spiritual ways is to incorporate spiritual values into everyday life. Formal practices – e.g., sitting meditation, mindfulness yoga or tai chi – are thus methods that help us to experience and live love, peacefulness and the awareness of deep meaning throughout the daily routine. Living out this love in everyday life – in acting, thinking and feeling, and with every passing moment – is not easy and needs to be practised with total dedication, patience and perseverance. This is true even for those who have found the deep meaning, the peace and absolute love, through the practice of object-free meditation. With the gift of the experience of this new reality, the spiritual path has only just begun. The experience described in the preceding chapters thus denotes not only the pinnacle but also the starting point of the spiritual path.[111]

On the other hand, I can strive to live spiritual values in everyday life independent of the kind of experiences I have gained on my path of object-free meditation. To live for these values should be from the outset the most important aim – apart from regular practice. This chapter is therefore directed at everyone who currently walks the spiritual path – regardless of whether for a day or ten years. This is also what Krishnamurti means to express when he says that there is no path that leads to the spiritual reality. The spiritual reality is what now *is*.[112] As of the first step, you are on the path – and not only after having met a certain objective that corresponds to our idea of it or the ideas of our teachers. Everyone who sets forth on this path has never and now reached the true and definite destination with respect to living spiritual values in everyday life.

Mindfulness is central to the incorporation of spiritual values

All spiritual ways have the fact in common that mindfulness – living mindfully in the present moment – is of prime importance when incorporating spiritual values into everyday life. There are exercises that help us to be mindful during the daily routine. Short moments of respite, for instance – a time-out when we return our focus to breathing, the body and the present moment – or the mindful performance of a routine task (e.g. taking a shower). Valuable advice regarding such exercises in mindfulness in everyday life can be found in the books by Jon Kabat-Zinn and Thich Nhat Hanh.

Mindfulness in everyday life also entails clearly seeing one's own self

To live mindfully also means to clearly perceive the self – with all its thoughts, feelings, features and desires. [113]

The direct experience of the spiritual reality opens up a new world to the meditating person, where love for everyone and everything prevails and guides him or her to a new life. Admittedly, this new life might not look very different when viewed from the outside. It remains the life of human existence on this earth – with all its pleasant and unpleasant experiences. In a Zen story, the recently enlightened monk shoulders his bundle – which he had just been able to set aside thanks to his enlightenment – anew.[114] The newly born Christian, after having become free from himself, 'takes up his cross daily'.[115]

For this is the most important practice in everyday life: to mindfully *carry* our *self* with all its features. However, we do this not with the aim to suppress bad, inferior or wicked thoughts, feelings or fantasies – or to change the *self* or to attempt to *better* oneself. [116] It is also not about condemning ourselves because of what we perceive as our *self*. Mindfulness means to clearly perceive the features of our *self* and its effect on our everyday life – without distortion but with acceptance and love.

Only a clear and undistorted perception of our conscious and unconscious drives, instincts, urges and fears can lead to a genuine change. We practise this undistorted perception during object-free meditation. Whenever we stay with ourselves in silence – without anything standing in between, without a wall concealing something, without distorting reality by means of embellishment – we clearly see what and how we are. Regular practice returns us to this point of orientation time and again – a point that allows us to identify values and priorities in the course of our existence as human beings anew. Moreover, regular practice heightens the sensitivity of our perceptions of our own internal world – it improves our ability to discern the stirrings of our emotions as reactions to external and internal events and situations.

This *knowledge* or *competence* – the undistorted perception of our *self* – represents one of the most important insights on the spiritual path. The profundity of this realisation therefore also represents a measure for spiritual maturity. The realisation that everything which I condemn in others – from selfishness and arrogance to malice and violence – everything that I see in the external world where hatred, war and violence cause endless suffering, is also part of myself and I a part of it.

Perceiving without distortion, without any embellishments, can only come from the stillness of the moment – free from self-centred desires, from wanting to be better than others, free from my largely unconscious conditioning that judges everything I think of myself according to learnt paradigms. From the stillness of the moment, I am able to lovingly accept everything without judgement. This seeing with the eyes of love – which embellishes nothing and condemns nothing – allows us to gently deal with our *self* – with ourselves as human beings who have grown up and live in this world – with love and humility. It allows us to shoulder our *self,* every day and every moment anew.

I cannot change my own self by deliberate efforts

By seeing clearly, we become aware of this truth time and again: I cannot change myself – meaning volitionally on the conscious plane. I can overcome myself. I can swiftly suppress my – by means of heredity and personal development – deeply rooted characteristics, the instincts, the anger and the hatred that arise from within me. I may even be able to deny their existence and keep them from entering the conscious plane. I am able to block them out of my mind. This does not make me a better person, but perhaps makes my behaviour even more arrogant and artificial. Denial of those inner features – which I denigrate and condemn – brings with it the danger of projecting them outwards – onto the *evil others* – with all the consequences of conflict and violence.

Every attempt to change our selves is largely motivated by the desire to display our *self* as better than it actually is. This desire distorts our gaze. We see ourselves – after having mentally decided to not do something any more or to do it differently in the future – in a better light and not how we really are. For this very reason, all our resolutions are to be examined with regards to whether or not they cloud our view. If a change or improvement truly ought to take place, then it has to happen on the unconscious plane.

This requirement, though, is not to be understood in the sense that I should uncontrollably live out my dark side in order not to suppress it. On the contrary, I should constantly consciously strive to live love and not hurt other people with my unbridled conduct – even when I feel an inner urge to burst out in emotion or violence. I should not make this change thinking that it was to make me a better human being or that this dark side was not a part of me, but knowing that my dark side will remain as such – that my urges remain urges, that my hatred remains hatred, that my fear remains fear. Only by seeing without distortions – by accepting and carrying my *self*, as it is – am I able to free myself from it. To deny its existence, to flee from it or to fight it, is of no help.

Contact with other people is invaluable to our attempts to clearly detect our characteristics. We only become aware of many characteristics in our relationships with partners, colleagues, friends or relatives, whether because of their remarks about our behaviour or our own responses to the behaviour of others. A Buddhist master is supposed to have said: 'If someone's behaviour keeps bothering you for more than ten minutes then you should look for the answer within yourself and not in the other person.'

Complete acceptance – carrying the cross (as it is phrased in Christianity) or the bundle (as it is told in the Zen story) – is the only way to liberation. It cannot be stressed enough that the actual task in everyday life is not to improve through resolutions and discipline but to arrive at a clearer perception of our *self* – as it is in the present moment – and the realisation and acceptance of the fact that we are just as we are. It is a task that does not originate from resignation or desperation, but from friendly, loving attention.

To live out spiritual values in everyday life does not mean that man should not enjoy nice and pleasant perceptions – such as a work of art, a nice meal, an erotic experience, the beauty of nature, a friendship, a romantic relationship or the birth of a child. On the contrary, it heightens the experience of said joy. However, it can also be let go of again. Living mindfully in everyday life means that we do not cling to pleasant – also spiritual – experiences. It means that we are free from involuntary thoughts that it might be possible to prolong or intensify these experiences. It means learning to take them as they come and are, not as a substitute satisfaction for the yearning for the meaning of life and absolute acceptance and love. This yearning resides, consciously or unconsciously, within most human beings and the substitute satisfaction of it is often found to be the cause of addictive behaviour.

Conversely, a similar statement can be made regarding unpleasant events. The act of perception – the experience of negative feelings caused by disappointment, for instance – is even intensified compared to people who do not meditate. The painful or otherwise unpleasant events are, however, perceived as such – as part of our existence in this world – and can thus be accepted and let go of.

Regular meditation practice gives the strength and lays the groundwork needed for spiritual growth.

In order to live mindfully every day – in order to carry our *self* and perceive it in an undistorted way – man needs to experience emptiness and stillness as the source of love and happiness, every day anew. This is the practice of unconditionally relinquishing everything, of residing solely in the present moment – in the now – in the stillness beyond thoughts and emotions, beyond all knowledge and all concepts. [117] All teachings and texts serve merely as a marker, signpost, on the road. They do not exist for us to stay with them but to show us the direction in which we are able to proceed on our path. We tend to attempt time and again, based on the teachings, to get to the spiritual dimension on the rational plane – with a concept, with our mind, with our *self.* The fact that this is not possible represents the main realisation and message of all major spiritual ways. The *self,* the reason, cannot be taken along to the spiritual reality. Thoughts and feelings do not have access to this stillness. In this place – where love for everything and everyone is born – our self as identification with our thoughts and emotions ceases to exist.

This stillness that we experience in the practice of meditation cannot be forced or earned. It is neither merit nor reward but a gift. And as a gift it can only be received in humility. For this reason, humility increases along the path of object-free meditation alongside growing experience. Those who have progressed farthest on the way can be recognised by their humility. [118] The silent presence and humility – not particular concepts, beliefs or teachings – provide an opportunity for a true change in our demeanour and for experiencing the spiritual reality in everyday life. This is when the act of *carrying the self* – the bundle, the cross – is no longer perceived as a burden imposed on us, but as a free act stemming from the experiencing of the gift.

This is an important reason for the daily formal practice. It is not that we should attempt to preserve most of what we experience during meditation for our daily lives – for instance by summoning certain pleasant conditions or feelings from memory. The daily experience of meditation can grow into a mindful experiencing of everyday life on an unconscious level. It helps us to experience mundane moments, over and over again anew, as the present moment – as it is – without past (also without memories of experiences gained through meditation) and without future. As much as corn needs the sun in order to grow and ripen, we need the energy that we are able to gain from the inexhaustible source of stillness – as a gift, every day anew – for spiritual growth.

Passing on of information on spiritual values and the path of object-free meditation

The question of how extensively and in what way I actively inform other people about the spiritual path is very important. On one hand, we are only able to walk this path because we have been informed about it. On the other hand, proactively *missionising* can be misunderstood or even do more harm than good. This is why it is hard to give general advice on this topic. Everybody has to find his or her own answer to the question. As an illustration of this search that will perhaps also help the reader to adopt an attitude, here is the personal account of a student of meditation describing the motivation for and the difficulties faced in connection with this activity:

For some years, the meaning and aim of my life has been clear and present to me: to increase love. Writing this, I am very much aware that this might sound banal, cheesy, naïve or presumptuous to people who have not experienced all-encompassing love as the source and aim of being. I found peace, deep meaning and love nearly ten years ago after having practised object-free meditation for a long time. I, and the whole of what I perceive during my existence as a human being, am enveloped in this love. It had simply been the most important experience of my life. Soon thereafter, it became my first priority to increase love by means of my life – my actions and my behaviour. I automatically adopted this attitude, as a consequence of this experience, without anyone having encouraged or asked me to do so.

For a very long time I thought that to pass on the information about the spiritual path was the most effective way to increase love. After experiencing the spiritual dimension, as the most important thing that man is allowed to experience during his existence in this world, it seemed self-evident to talk to as many people as possible about the path leading to this experience. Not because of having become someone who wants to 'put other people right', who sees himself as being more or better than others due to having attained something others do not know about. I simply wanted to share this experience of an all-encompassing love with all people.

Similarly perhaps to someone who seeks to show other people – who live in the fog, who are freezing and psychologically and physically ill due to the lack of light – a path that leads them out of this sea of fog where they are able to reach a place bathed in sunlight with ample space for everyone. The path may be rocky and long, it may lead through dark forest, through thicket, gorges, dry deserts and at times it might even look like there is not even a path. Having reached the destination, each and every one knows that he or she had to go towards this light, even if the path had been ten times longer and even more burdensome.

Or as someone who lives in the desert with others, where most people are constantly dying of thirst but merely have contaminated water at their disposal that, after having been consumed, will only cause a bigger thirst and diseases. As someone who has, after an extensive search, found a source of pure, clear water that allows people to quench their thirst and the purity of which causes recovery from many illnesses.

I also wanted to share the information about the path leading to the experience of the spiritual dimension because I saw the only chance for humanity as a whole to be saved from this spiral of violence and destruction to be by means of an encounter of individual people with this dimension of love. A change in this development – the destruction and mutilation of fellow human beings and the environment with ever more efficient means of violence – is only possible if particular people are able to renounce violence. Mahatma Ghandi said: 'Peace between countries must rest on the solid foundation of love between individuals.'

With much joy and energy I set to work, proclaiming this 'good news' both for every individual as well as the whole of humankind. I compiled PowerPoint slides, flyers, brochures and websites detailing this – from my point of view – most significant information that man can be given during his existence in this world. To my surprise, I had to realise that most people did not care about my piece of information – be it because they were too busy with their lives, be it because they did not believe it to be true or did not listen to me, be it because they thought that they should not have to be lectured to or because the tribulations along the path discouraged them.

Yet, there were also ailing people who were longing for light and good health. Having reached them, I had to realise that most of them had already tried several different paths and that they had – by way of a book store and advertisements on the internet – received the offer to purchase many other, interesting, shorter and possibly painless solutions for their suffering. To the sufferers and the searchers, my piece of information was just one out of several hundred offers and not 'the' way.

I was deeply disappointed. I sought additional possibilities to pass on this relevant information (i.e. lectures for interested parties, organising group meditation) and had to realise that, in addition to the lack of interest, my limited abilities to attractively express myself in speech and writing in order to convince others, were a barrier. Many people, who had experienced the same thing as I had, had described this path more skilfully in books and lectures than I was capable of doing. At that point, I wasn't sure any longer whether my endeavours to inform others was the appropriate activity to increase love.

A few years ago, I suddenly realised that there is only one possibility to make sure that a specific act (behaviour or activity) increases love: to act out of love. The most effective 'proclamation' is not made by means of nice words and images, but with appropriate attitude and action. This is also how the quotation by Lao Tzu can be read: 'Who knows does not speak.' Similarly speaks Mahatma Gandhi the famous imperative: 'Be the change that you want to see in the world.' This realisation corresponds with what many spiritual teachers – for instance Buddha, Jesus, Augustine, Meister Eckhart, Johannes Tauler, Francis of Assisi, Jiddu Krishnamurti – have said.

But how do I act out of love? How do I know if my actions actually increase love? How do I know if an action ostensibly stemming from love might not just follow my ego – which likes to think of itself as a do-gooder, a helper, as someone better than other people? The fact that my ego strives for exactly that, I know based on my self-observation during meditation and in everyday life during times of mindfulness. From this experience, I also know that my ego – in its longstanding conditioning – can only be changed very slowly. I know too that, based on my psychological knowledge, I am only conscious of a fragment of 'my shadow' – the part of my person that I, my ego, condemn, does not accept and therefore often suppresses. How do I thus know that I am not causing more harm than love with my 'well-intentioned' actions? I have said or done many a well-meant thing which has led to rage, anger, envy, inferiority complexes and other forms of suffering.

The answer is the following for me: I am able to act out of love, if I am connected with love – the plane of being where I am kept. I am able to come into contact with this plane, if I withdraw from the noise of my thoughts and external events – if I meditate. This aforementioned connection established by means of meditation also has its effect on everyday life. The more I am in contact with this plane, the more easily and often I am able to encounter and connect to it in everyday life. To me, this entails living 'mindfully', 'consciously' or 'awakened'. Being conscious of this plane that is always there. In no way might this entail being out of touch with reality. On the contrary, if I am living mindfully and consciously, then I see everything much more clearly as it is – then I see with the eyes of love. Including my ego with all its thoughts and feelings.

June 2012

Appendix 1:
The Spiritual Dimension

WHAT IS THE SPIRITUAL DIMENSION?

Throughout our lifetimes on this earth, humans have to develop skills at various interwoven and mutually influencing levels to survive as individuals and as a species: the physical, intellectual, social, creative, spiritual, etc.

In Western culture today, the most highly developed of these levels is the intellectual or rational level, which is based on a scientific and materialistic view of the world. Using reason, humans can gain knowledge about the objects of their surroundings, describe them and successfully use or control them to their advantage. Thus, in Western culture, this level is often considered the most important one, or perhaps even the only one that matters.

Some important factors of human existence do, however, elude the purely rational mind. These include factors that are of existential significance for the individual and for humankind as a whole, such as ethics, morals and the meaning of life. Karl Popper, a leading philosopher of the 20th century, is in fact of the opinion that every rational discussion or act, including natural science, presupposes ethical principles that are not comprehensible on a purely rational level.[119] These ethical and moral foundations of our thinking processes, which lie beyond rational comprehension, have their roots in the spiritual dimension. The immediate experience of ethical and moral principles and of a profound meaning of human life is possible only in the spiritual dimension.

Women and men have given accounts of their experience of the spiritual dimension for over 2500 years. In his book, *Perennial Philosophy*,[120] an anthology of writings describing these experiences, Aldous Huxley refers to 'eternal truths', which women and men continue to experience to this day. This reality has been given many names through the centuries (e.g. God, the Absolute, the Void, the spiritual dimension, the mystical dimension, intuition), but ultimately is and remains nameless, because it lies beyond what our reason can comprehend and describe in words. Because of its effect, it could perhaps best be described as love.

The earliest reports of this experience known to us can be traced back to religion. But we could also claim that, on the contrary, the experience of the spiritual dimension was the origin of religion. Those who had experienced it attempted to convey it to others. This is how different religions developed a long time ago, most of them over 2000 years ago. Although they differ in terms of how they describe the experience, they all draw from the same source.

These eternal truths are independent of time and of religious teachings. They can be found in sacred writings of different religions: in the Upanishads of Hinduism, in the teachings of Buddha and in the Bible. The Dalai Lama says, 'Since love is at the core of all religions, we could speak of a universal religion of love.'[121] At the level of mysticism, the level of a personal path to a religious experience, we find more similarities in religions than differences.

Why do humans today not see the eternal truths of our human existence in the sacred religious texts and in the writings of contemporary spiritual scholars who describe this dimension, and instead see mostly contradictions? Why is much of what is written there not compatible with our logical thinking? Why do we get confused when we try to understand these writings with our reason?

We read in these writings and hear from individuals who have experienced it that the spiritual dimension is in fact our true self; that the foundation not only of our selves but of the entire cosmos – that the very source of our being, which in the Christian tradition is referred to as God – is love. We read in the New Testament of the Bible: *God is love.*[122] However, when we look at our life and the lives of many other humans as well as at the lives of other living beings, we see suffering, misfortune, the struggle for life and for survival, violence and cruelty. If God is love, why is there so much suffering in this world?

At the rational level, when we use logical reason, we realise that the different religious teachings contradict each other as well. Contradictions exist even within each religion. For example, when we read the gospels of the New Testament, the stories (or 'facts') in each of the four gospels often differ. When we try to comprehend it at the rational level, we get confused.

We are confused because these writings speak of a dimension of our existence that lies beyond the boundary of rational comprehension. Mystics, but also different philosophers, have emphasised time and again that we are incapable of reaching by means of reason the dimension of meaning and describing it in logical sentences.

Ludwig Wittgenstein, one of the greatest logicians and philosophers of the last century, describes the limits of reason using the metaphor of the red glass bell.[123] We are trapped in this glass bell, and everything we see appears red. Only once we break through the glass do we realise that the light is not actually red, but colourless. As soon as we return to the glass bell, to the space that lies within the boundary of reason, we cannot prove that the light is not actually red because underneath this bell, everything appears to be coloured red. Plato's allegory of the cave is a similar metaphor.

The experience of the spiritual dimension cannot be adequately described in words. The spiritual dimension lies beyond our rational comprehension. Trying to understand it can be compared to living in a two-dimensional world and trying to look at three-dimensional objects.

The picture represents a three-dimensional object in the plane; that is, it is represented in two dimensions. We recognise that it is a chair, an object from the three-dimensional world. However, we can only identify it as such because we are looking at it from the three-dimensional space perspective, which we are only capable of doing because we live in a three-dimensional world. If we lived in a two-dimensional world (in the plane), we would only see meaningless lines.

Here is another picture of a chair, depicted from two perspectives, from the side and from the front:

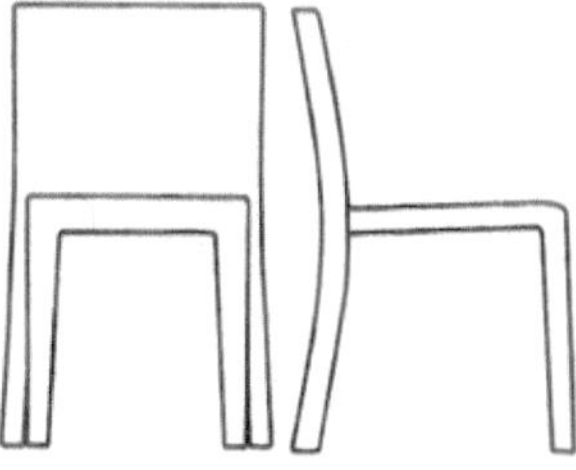

We can make a synthesis of these two illustrations and thus recognise that it is two separate depictions of the same three-dimensional object. We are capable of doing this only because we have seen objects in three-dimensional space before.

Figuratively speaking, our reason exists in a two-dimensional world to which the third dimension, the spiritual one, is alien. Our reason sees only lines; viewed from the perspective of logical thinking, physical bodies and three-dimensional objects do not exist. 'Objects' from the three-dimensional – from the spiritual – space are therefore incomprehensible for us. When individuals who have experienced the spiritual dimension describe it in words, our reason perceives their reports as contradictory.

Only those individuals who have experienced the three-dimensional space recognise such objects in the descriptions. That first picture therefore makes sense to them. It is not made up of chaotic lines. But logical reasoning, which knows only the two-dimensional world, cannot understand it.

The Spiritual Path

We cannot access the spiritual dimension through reason. Even if we let someone convince us that it is real, the descriptions do not make sense to us. The only way to gain access to this dimension is to experience it for ourselves. This does not take place at the rational level.

Every human has the ability – at least a seminal ability – to experience the spiritual level giving meaning to human existence. This ability is often perceived as a notion of the eternal or the meaningful, as a longing for love. When this seed is cultivated, it is possible to break out of the two-dimensional plane, through the red glass bell.

Most people in today's world cannot cultivate this seed without help. We have been raised in a world in which rational thinking is considered the highest authority for knowing what is truth. Figuratively speaking, the world exists only within the red glass bell. We are bombarded with this way of thinking every day.

One spiritual path – figuratively speaking, a tool that helps us break the red glass bell, break out of the two-dimensional world – is the practice of object-free meditation described in this book. It helps us recognise that light is not red, that objects have three dimensions, that a dimension exists that lies beyond the boundary of the rational one. That is why we speak of awakening. We suddenly become aware of more and realise that what we can understand with our reason is not all there is.

It takes time and regular practice to see that we are more than our thoughts, to experience the space of stillness in which thoughts and emotions are suspended; the stillness, in which I[124] can encounter the touch of the spiritual dimension, in which, expressed in religious terms, I can 'listen to God'.

When everything is still, we can perceive the eternal, the all-encompassing, we can experience that love is the fundamental source of our being. The Bible says *God is love* and Krishnamurti asserts, 'There is no silence without love.'[125] When something else is present – fear, discontent, sorrow, desire for liberation, for freedom – thoughts and emotions are also always present, and there is no stillness. The practice of object-free meditation guides us to the stillness.

Once we have experienced stillness, the spiritual and religious writings no longer seem alien to us. We recognise the 'three-dimensional space' in the writings, which consists of far more than what the words we read with our reason can actually convey.

These writings can then help us on our path to the nameless, to the fundamental source of our being. We then also recognise that the writings have many commonalities. Even though they look very different from the outside, since they stem from different individuals and religious traditions, we realise that they all allude to and bring us closer to the spiritual dimension, to the 'three-dimensional world' mentioned in the metaphor above.

In our culture, these writings stem primarily from the Christian tradition. Those who do not have an aversion or bear resentment towards the Christian religion – caused perhaps by negative experiences with the official Church – do not need to turn to Eastern religions for help. There are numerous writings by Christian mystics which can be used in the same way, as a guide on the path of object-free meditation.

The most renowned writings come from the late Middle Ages and the early days of the modern era. In the German-speaking region, the main ones are the writings of Meister Eckhart[126] and Johannes Tauler.[127] *The Cloud of Unknowing*[128] – a manuscript by an anonymous author written in Middle English – and the writings of the Spanish mystic St John of the Cross accompany us on our spiritual path to this day.

Although the authors describe the path to 'Theosis' or 'union with God' differently, they have much in common. It is what they have in common in particular that can help us today on our spiritual path of object-free meditation.

One thing that we find mentioned in all descriptions is the emptiness, the stillness without content, or the nothingness.

Meister Eckhart says: 'You cannot do better than to place yourself in darkness and in unknowing. (...)Now you might say, "Oh sir, (...) if a man is in such a state of pure nothingness, is it not better to do something to beguile the gloom and desolation, such as praying or listening to sermons (...)?" No, be sure of this. Absolute stillness for as long as possible is best of all for you.'[129]

The author of the *Cloud of Unknowing* writes to a friend: 'Leave aside this everywhere and this everything, in exchange for this nowhere and this nothing.'[130]

We also find this call to abide with nothingness, in stillness, in Hinduism and Buddhism. A Zen master, Shunryu Suzuki, who founded a Zen centre in San Francisco at the end of the 1960s, articulates it in simple terms: 'We have to go through the gate of emptiness.'[131]

As the name suggests, object-free meditation guides us to this emptiness, to this stillness, to this nothingness.

Nothingness

Why do I find God[132] only in nothingness? Because God is an absolute foothold. As long as I find my footing in 'something', as long as I'm holding on to anything – be it the most trivial or the most sacred thing – I am still attached to 'something'. And each 'something' is subject to change, is impermanent, cannot provide a foothold which is independent of the circumstances and of my psychic conditions. God is what remains when everything else fails.[133] To experience God, I have to first experience that everything else fails. I will be able to see the impermanence of everything when I linger in the emptiness, in the nothingness, using a practice that leads me to the emptiness.

This path can be difficult and painful.[134] It is not about renouncing pleasure, about asceticism, but about surrendering that which gives me footing. That is why John of the Cross refers to the practice of contemplation (which is what object-free meditation is called in Christian mysticism) as dark night.[135] To experience the absolute foothold, I have to surrender all.

Rationally, at the level of reason, I can understand and relate to the sentence *God is the absolute foothold, that which remains when all else fails.* Such rational understanding, however, is only a thought. I can only <u>experience</u> God as absolute foothold if I surrender everything else. That is painful, but the suffering – regardless of how difficult it may seem – is nothing compared to what I gain: the absolute foothold, the source of goodness, of love, which gives meaning to my life and to the entirety in which I live as a human being.

Thoughts come and go, memories change. An immediate experience of this solid ground, the feeling of being securely kept in love, remains. That is why Meister Eckhart asserts 'A man should not have, or be satisfied with, an imagined God, for then, when the idea vanishes, God vanishes! Rather, one should have an essential God, who far transcends the thought of man and all creatures.'[136]

This foothold is independent of the given circumstances, of the situation in which I live and most notably, is independent of myself. I know this because the experience comes as a gift, something that I – my will, my individual self – cannot precipitate. I can only use my will to decide to take the path which, according to many people's reports, will guide me to this experience. A path that, one could say, makes me receptive to this experience. When and how I get this gift is beyond the control of my will and my knowledge.

According to the Gospel of John, Jesus says: 'The wind blows where it wishes, and you hear its sound, but you do not know where it comes from or where it goes. So it is with everyone who is born of the Spirit.'[137] In a lecture Krishnamurti said: 'You cannot invite the wind but you must leave the window open.'[138]

Object-free meditation is a path to this experience; it is not the only one, but it is a reliable and direct path. It helps me recognise that my thoughts are thoughts and that my emotions are emotions, that I am not identical and do not have to identify with them. It helps me realise that everything that gives me footing – be it material objects such as money or ideational ones such as recognition – is fleeting and subject to change, and can therefore not provide an absolute foothold. Regular practice of object-free meditation leads me to the place where I can experience an absolute foothold, the spiritual dimension of my existence, my true self.

The path requires full commitment, resilience and strength. I need commitment to be able to surrender everything that gives me footing, and this is necessary for the practice's effect to fully unfold. Only the practice exists while I am practising: the breathing, the stillness. We could say today: I must fully and unconditionally engage in the practice. I must be fully involved – physically, mentally and with my heart.

Commitment also implies respect, piety and humility. Aware that I am approaching a space where I can encounter an absolute ground – the Absolute itself – my full attention and love is focused on the practice. Everything is part of it – my thoughts, my emotions, my body – everything is part of it, fully focused on the practice, by means of focusing on breathing, which is my anchor. My breathing – perhaps coupled with a word that I utter to myself with every breath – helps me be here in the now, in this very moment, and to not let myself be distracted by external events or thoughts and emotions that arise from within me.

I might think, 'I can focus on my breathing and be fully and unconditionally involved but without commitment and humility.' However, without commitment, I cannot be fully involved; instead I am rooted in my own self, which is not participating in the practice.

We find the description of full and unconditional commitment in the writings of Christian mystics as well as in Eastern religions.

A few quotes:

In the Gospel of Matthew, Jesus says, 'If anyone would come after me, let him deny himself and take up his cross and follow me.'[139]

Ayya Khema, a German-speaking Buddhist nun and spiritual teacher, asserts, 'If we cannot surrender at least temporarily, it is impossible to stop thinking [...] But the moment we are willing to surrender ourselves, meditation becomes possible.'[140]

In Bhagavad Gita, one of Hinduism's most important canonical scriptures, Krishna, the incarnation of the highest God, says to the hero Arjuna: 'But by single-minded devotion, O Arjuna, I may [...] be known and seen.'[141]

These and other writings originating from the religious tradition can be of great assistance on the spiritual path.

Some view religious teachings, the context in which these manuscripts were written, as an obstacle. For these women and men, it will be good to hear that the path of object-free meditation can also be embarked upon independently of any religious concepts. Three such perspectives describing the path of object-free meditation that are independent of all religious teachings are presented in this book.

However, a path independent of religious teachings will also pass through emptiness. I also need to leave everything behind to experience the absolute foothold and absolute peace. And this path may also lead through difficult phases.

When I regularly practise object-free meditation for a certain period of time, my attitude changes. I see my thoughts and emotions more clearly and without glossing over them. I notice that I develop impulses which I generally condemn in others and usually suppress, and I become aware that hardly any thoughts or emotions exist that cannot arise in me as well. This realisation can be painful.

If I continue the practice, I progressively realise that my consciousness behind or between these thoughts and emotions is empty. There are moments in which even my own self seems insubstantial. I sit here in front of and together with the emptiness. This path through the emptiness, the nothingness, is difficult and can generate fear.

At the same time, the practice of meditation also strengthens my mental stability through daily self-reflection, the perception of my inner self and the awareness of my emotions and thoughts. Time and again I experience the space of stillness, in which everything is suspended; it gives me footing.

As is the case when embarking on the religious path, continuing the practice despite the difficult experiences is only possible when the individual is fully committed. Only when I am prepared to let everything go can I continue down the path. If I continue to practise regularly, I will eventually come to experience my true self. I learn that I am one with the emptiness with which I abide during the meditation – the emptiness which encloses everything and in which everything resides. I am like a wave looking into the depths of an immeasurable and bottomless ocean and realising that it is part of that ocean.

Through this encounter, I experience the deeper meaning of life, freedom, joy and love for everything and everyone. Myself, all humans, everything that drives us as human beings, is suspended in love. In this way, object-free meditation is a spiritual path, even when it is practised independent of any religious teaching.

Independent of what guides me when practising object-free meditation, the experience of the spiritual dimension cannot be described in words. Each description, and thus also the words written above, falls short and represents a distorted picture. Coming to know the spiritual dimension requires a personal path, one's own immediate experience. This 'knowledge' cannot be conveyed with words at the level of reason.

Integration into Daily Life[142]

My attitude in everyday life changes with the experiences I have on the spiritual path. It is increasingly affected by my will to act in everyday life in accordance with my inner attitude – namely with the ethical values whose source I have experienced.

I then realise, however, that I do not always – perhaps most of the time I do not – succeed in living out these spiritual values, most notably love, in everyday life. I need help, a crutch. Just as during meditation the focus on my breathing functions as a crutch to stay with the present moment, I need a crutch in everyday life as well, which I can intentionally turn to.

Such a crutch in everyday life can be commandments such as *You shall love your neighbour as yourself.*[143] But more beneficial than commandments is a concept from which an ethical attitude towards others basically evolves on its own. Contrary to our mind-set during meditation – when we surrender all concepts and sit with the emptiness, focusing on our breath – concepts in everyday life that I can intentionally turn to at the rational level can be quite useful.

One concept the author finds appealing and which helps him in everyday life is described by the great French philosopher and mystic Simone Weil, in her essay entitled 'Draft for a Statement of Human Obligations'.[144]

She refers to her concept, which she describes at the beginning of the essay, as *Profession of Faith*. The profession begins with the ascertainment that an absolute good – we could call it absolute love – exists outside the materialistic level that we can perceive with our senses. People cannot grasp this reality with our senses, nor with reason.

In each human being, this reality corresponds to the longing for an absolute good. A link to this extramundane reality can grow from this seed. In this way, a part of the good can flow into our world.

This seed is present in every human being. According to Simone Weil, because of the existence of this seed and the resulting possibility to establish a link with the absolute good, each human being, without exception, is sacred, and we are therefore obligated to pay respect and reverence to her or him. In her profession of faith, Simone Weil states: 'All human beings are absolutely identical in so far as they can be thought of as consisting of a centre, which is an unquenchable desire for good, surrounded by an accretion of psychical and bodily matter.'[145]

If I realise this, I then am left with no choice but to treat each fellow human being with veneration, with respect, and to wish each human being well. Such a concept, if believed, when experienced as an inner truth, leads to the development of an ethical attitude towards all other humans.

The concept describes the same phenomenon that the metaphor about the wave and the ocean conveys. When we encounter the spiritual dimension on our path of object-free meditation, we are like the wave that touches the ocean when it looks into its depths. Not only does it thereby become aware of its own immeasurable depth, but it also realises that other waves arise from that same ocean, that they all *are* this ocean. This experience leads to a change in attitude towards myself and towards all other human beings.

The Dalai Lama means the same when he says: 'Regardless of whether or not we belong to a religion, we all have a fundamental and profoundly human wellspring of ethics within ourselves. We need to nurture that shared ethical basis. (...) More integral than religion is our fundamental human spirituality – that is the affinity we humans have for love, benevolence, and affection – no matter what religion we belong to.'[146]

It could, however, be argued that the concepts described in the writings of Simone Weil and the Dalai Lama, and the metaphor about the wave and the ocean, point out something important and beautiful. They are appealing, and I experience them in meditation as well. In everyday life, however, my ego speaks out – with reactions of frustration and fear, with the pursuit of prestige or retaliation, with the perception of others as competitors or perhaps even as foes.

Does a remedy exist? Yes: mindfulness.

Mindfulness in everyday life first and foremost means to clearly perceive my self. To see my reactions which are co-determined by my predisposition, my childhood upbringing and my life experiences – I may have suffered severe abuse during childhood.

Mindfulness also means to refrain from judging. If I condemn myself for one of my reactions – a thought, an emotion, an action – then I am not being mindful; it is my ego that reacts. My ego strives to be a good human being, and frustration, anger, gloating, envy, power hunger are not characteristics of good people. Mindfulness in everyday life means clearly perceiving my self without judgement.

If I find myself reacting to frustration, anger or hostility, it may help to visualise the concept of Simone Weil's profession of faith. I then become aware that my wife or husband, my sister, my father-in-law, my boss, the dissatisfied customer, the poor sport on my team who keeps criticising my good ideas, and I, too – despite the fact that I might well up in exasperation or anger – am a being along with all others, in whom a seed lies that wants to and that can connect with the good.

I realise that each human being, and thus also the individual that I am talking to now or thinking about – and hence also I myself – is sacred, surrounded by physical matter and by features that can be perceived from the outside – even when my impression is that that individual's behaviour cannot be considered sacred.

Perceiving my reactions and envisioning Simone Weil's concept or the wave metaphor *directly* helps in situations when I enter into a relationship with another human being.

There are three tools that *indirectly* support us in everyday life. They all strengthen our ability to be mindful in everyday life. The change in our attitude occurs when we implement them, mostly without our even realising it.

Experience shows that the first and most important of these three tools is daily sessions of sitting meditation. Twenty minutes or more, preferably in the morning, before we start our daily routine, sitting with our breathing, in the emptiness. The effect, as already mentioned, is not immediately observable, and also not on the first day. It might even happen that I am more irritated or more sensitive after the meditation, that I respond with stronger emotions than before.

If we practise regularly, our ability to be mindful in everyday life increases with time. I perceive my reactions more frequently and more clearly, without having to understand or explain them, and keep discovering new ones at an even deeper and even less conscious level – even after 20 years of meditation. This is a lifelong task and journey of discovery.

When I practise regularly, my ability to refrain from judging also improves. In everyday life I become aware more quickly that the goal is *perceiving* rather than *judging* – perceiving with loving attention.

The second tool for strengthening mindfulness in everyday life is the mindful performance of routine tasks. In addition to regular sessions of sitting meditation in the morning, I can aim to be mindful every time I take a shower, brush my teeth or walk to the bus stop, by conscientiously carrying out the movements and being aware of my sensations during this activity. This exercise is similar to mindful walking during a meditation course.

Finally, in addition to meditation in the morning, we can set aside a few times a day 3 to 5 minutes for mindfulness exercises at work. In a place where I know that I will not be disturbed, I can focus on my breathing, become aware of my body, my thoughts, my emotions and impulses, and then return to my breathing, and stay with this focus until the end of the time window. [147]

The daily practice of sitting meditation and the two other exercises do more than strengthen my ability to be mindful in everyday life. Regular practice makes me become aware more frequently and with more clarity of the stillness in which everything is suspended. I then also experience this space of stillness or emptiness as the space of love. It is a reality that prevails, independent from what I do or think – a reality that at any given moment can be filled anew with meaning and love.

Appendix 2:
Believing and Knowing

This addendum serves as an attempt to describe two concepts – *experience* or *knowing* on one side and *belief* or *trust* on the other – that are, implicitly or explicitly, used throughout the text of this book. The book appeals to the *belief* or the *trust* of the readers to set forth on a path that will lead them to *knowing* or *experience*.

The terms *knowledge* and *belief* can – very much like most words – mean several things. There are countless writings that define them much more precisely than the discourse at hand.

Nevertheless, the author sees fit to attempt to analyse them with regards to their meaning – as he has interpreted them. Within our western culture, with its religious, philosophical and scientific (based on our reason and logical thinking) tradition, the terms have been burdened with much imagery and prejudice. By making clear what these two words signify to him, the author hopes to help the reader come to a better understanding of the notion the book tries to convey.

EXPERIENCE

Experience refers to what I perceive, witness and undergo. It is the first-hand awareness of both external and internal events. Experience takes place immediately during the act of perceiving or witnessing an event. An experience needs to be retrievable from memory for me to be able to remember and refer to it.

It may be self-evident that experience constitutes a very minor part (a lot less than a hundred thousandth for instance) of all the events that take place in my surroundings and inner self (both my corporeal and psychic inner selves) at a given time. Thus, it would be pretentious to assert that an event had not taken place or an object not existed, simply because I have never observed it.

What exactly I experience – am consciously aware of – depends both on my cognitive abilities and on my stance. If I keep my eyes half shut, or am wearing ear plugs, then my cognitive abilities with regards to visual or auditory occurrences are reduced. The same goes for instances when I am only half awake, barely alert or under the influence of alcohol or other substances. Yet, even when I am alert, it can happen that I do not perceive something important – when, for instance, my attention is directed at something else. Many magic tricks rely on this fact by skilfully diverting our attention from the events that would reveal the trick in question.

When I experience something, I do not need to ask myself whether I believe it or not. When I see a red crayon on the table, I know – I immediately experience – that I am observing a crayon. Provided I am awake and mentally sane, then another person – who is also awake, not visually impaired and mentally sane – will perceive the same crayon when standing in the same place and having the same point of view. It does not constitute a matter of belief for myself nor for the other person, but a matter of experience.

The same holds true for internal events. When I experience them, I know that they are there and that I perceive them. If I – for instance – feel joy, then I know this to be true and do not have to believe in the fact that I am able to feel joy in the first place. I know this to be true, even though other people do not have access to the direct experience of this event – unlike with the crayon. Conversely, I do not have access to the internal events of other people. I do know, though, that I often laugh when feeling joy. When somebody laughs or expresses joy in another way, I am therefore able to infer from it that this person is feeling the same as I do when feeling joy. However, we are not able to directly experience the joy of another person as an object. We can merely experience its outcome.

Joy is not something we can point at and observe alongside one another – unlike the red crayon on the table. Only the individual that experiences it can directly perceive it. Nevertheless, I do not claim to believe in joy. I know, based on my direct experiences that I am able to feel joy and therefore do not have *to believe* that it exists. This certainty is most apparent when feeling joy.

Even at times when I do not feel joy, I nevertheless know that it exists based on my recollection of such an experience. The more dated my experience is, the fainter my recollection of and in turn *belief* in joy becomes. If I haven't felt joy for months, I still know of its existence but might not believe in being able to experience it any longer.

The same holds true for the *intensity* of feelings or a frame of mind. Even though I am aware – based on my experiences – that there are different levels of joy, I am only subjectively able to rate the intensity of joy at a specific point in time and only in comparison to my previous experiences. Most human beings know which experiences have provoked powerful emotions in the past. The most powerful of them overwhelm us. In that case, my conscious *self* may *dissolve* so that only this state exists. The more powerful and enduring the experience of a specific emotion, the more it leaves its mark on a human being. We remember especially intense experiences for a long time – they are quite often able to change our lives.

Direct perception is something I do not have to believe in because I know it to be true whilst perceiving it. Thus, the question is not whether I believe in it or not. If I am being honest with myself, I am able to know – in a state of being awake and sober – that a specific experience – be it a sensory perception or an emotional state – takes place. It is not a case of belief but of knowledge.

What exactly causes this experience is, without doubt, yet another question. When seeing a red crayon on the table, I assume that this crayon represents a material object. It might as well be that the crayon is merely an image or a hologram.

Internal events – thoughts, feelings and a specific emotional state – also raise questions concerning their causes and correlations. We know from research in psychology and psychotherapy that the internal correlations are often more complex than we think and that there are often many possible explanations for a specific emotional state – but we may not be able to determine with certainty which might be the correct or most probable one.

In contrast to the direct experience, as described above, with regards to the reasons and contexts that lead to an experience we are dependent on stories, concepts, theories and teachings; these – when we are not able to verify them by means of a direct experience – we must either believe, reject or (undecided) abandon. To what extent our view of the world in which we live is shaped by such stories and concepts – which we believe but have not verified ourselves or have not been able to verify – we do not know. It most probably amounts to quite a large amount, well over 90 per cent.

BELIEF

The word 'belief' is closely related to the verb 'believing' which – in everyday language – is often used as a way of expressing an opinion concerning a specific situation. As in: 'I believe he is still asleep', 'I believe he'll arrive before lunch time' or 'He doesn't believe he has forgotten to switch the light off in the cellar.' We use these sentences to express that we assume a specific event to be probable.

The sentence 'I believe in God' sometimes uses the verb 'believe' in the aforementioned sense: 'I believe in the existence of God.' However, there is a crucial difference. The believer doesn't regard it as probable but is certain that God exists, as much as the atheist believes that he or she knows for certain – and not as a mere probability – that God does not exist.

Believing in something we cannot verify by direct experience is part of our daily lives. For it would not even be possible to personally convince myself of everything all the time: that my wife really went shopping – as she said she would; that the 7:07 bus connection – which I take every day – is also on time today; that the cheese I am eating does not contain any harmful bacteria, etc. I do know, though, that the events – which I accept, which I believe to take place – are occurring or will occur, with varying levels of probability. Even though some are more likely – for instance that my bus leaves on time again today, especially since I live in Switzerland – there is no absolute certainty. Absolute certainty can only come with experience: When I see the bus arriving, I know for sure that it is on time today. This kind of *believing* means that it is possible to verify a subject and turn my belief into knowledge by means of direct experience.

How is it possible to *believe in God* – meaning to *believe* something that I cannot verify with absolute certainty? The rational human being cannot understand this because such an act contradicts reason. If somebody tells me that 1326 divided by 16 equals 82.875, then I may believe this person – but I will verify it myself before making the same claim in a discussion where other people have reached a different result. How can human beings – who are perfectly capable of using reason in their daily lives – take up this irrational attitude? We can deduce three possible reasons from the accounts of believers.

The *first* possibility is that man deliberately decides to believe in God – or, as an atheist, not to believe in God. A prominent example for such a decision can be found in *Pascal's Wager*. There, Blaise Pascal makes the following case:

> Let us then examine this point, and say, 'God is, or He is not.' But to which side shall we incline? Reason can decide nothing here. There is an infinite chaos which separated us. A game is being played at the extremity of this infinite distance where heads or tails will turn up.

What will you wager? According to reason, you can do neither the one thing nor the other; according to reason, you can defend neither of the propositions.

Do not then reprove for error those who have made a choice; for you know nothing about it. 'No, but I blame them for having made, not this choice, but a choice; for again both he who chooses heads and he who chooses tails are equally at fault, they are both in the wrong. The true course is not to wager at all.'

Yes; but you must wager. It is not optional. You are embarked. Which will you choose then? Let us see. Since you must choose, let us see which interests you least. You have two things to lose, the true and the good; and two things to stake, your reason and your will, your knowledge and your happiness; and your nature has two things to shun, error and misery. Your reason is no more shocked in choosing one rather than the other, since you must of necessity choose. This is one point settled. But your happiness? Let us weigh the gain and the loss in wagering that God is. Let us estimate these two chances. If you gain, you gain all; if you lose, you lose nothing. Wager, then, without hesitation that He is. [148]

Pascal argues that an analysis of the different options regarding the question of belief in God results in the following reasoning:

1. You believe in God, and God exists – in this case, you are being rewarded (Heaven – you have won).
2. You believe in God, and God does not exist – in this case, you have not won anything (but also not lost anything).
3. You do not believe in God, and God does not exist – in this case, you have not won anything either (but also not lost anything.)
4. You do not believe in God, and God exists – in this case, you are punished (Hell – you have lost).

From this analysis of the different possibilities, Pascal concludes that it was better to unconditionally believe in God.

Admittedly, this act of belief was much simpler for Pascal than for us today. We live in a multicultural society, in which not merely one but many religions invite us to believe in their religion or teachings – to believe in their *God* or *Gods*. For this reason, today's believer is aware of the fact that he may be regarded as a nonbeliever in the eyes of other believers who do not share the same confession of faith. Why does a human being decide to believe in certain scripts – written by human beings – as the absolute truth and to disregard others – which make a different claim – as falsehoods? Why choose one religion over another?

An answer to this question – why man comes to a decision that is so hard to justify by reason – could be that man decides in favour of a God because he needs a God.[149] That he considers the chosen religion to be the only valid one may be because many religions – either explicitly or implicitly – ask for this as part of their teachings.

Believing – because I have decided to do so – furthermore raises the question of whether I really do believe. Is man even able to force himself to unconditionally believe in something? Is it not in fact the case that I want to believe but simultaneously am not able to exclude certain doubts? Perhaps we should speak of a decision and explicit will to believe in the existence of God and certain dogmas and not of an unconditional belief. [150]

In addition to this belief in the existence of God, there are, *secondly*, people who believe in God in terms of trust. The belief in God, in that case, does not primarily consist of a belief in particular facts, but belief in the sense that I trust. [151] I trust in what people have reported or are reporting on regarding their experiences with God, without elevating their accounts to an absolute and concrete dogma. I place trust in the assumption that my life in this world is in good hands with God and I trust – I believe, I have faith – perhaps in a way that has been shown to me by people who have experienced God.

This point of view is less in contradiction to rational thinking, because trust or faith is not based on reason alone. It expresses and establishes itself not just in thinking and weighing probabilities on the rational level but also in feeling and in the overall attitude of a human being. I place my trust in what these people have given an account of. This path provides my life with support – a life where, when looked at rationally, absolute surety is missing. It is thus not about the belief in specific facts or dogmas, not about being part of an organisation, but about my personal attitude of trust. The trust in God is based on the trust in what other people report on. It normally presupposes a longing for surety – something that can keep me grounded, in which I can completely put my trust.

Often, a belief in dogmas is added to this. The people whose accounts a specific belief relies on are frequently part of religious or spiritual communities – most of whom have their own set of dogmas.

The *third* possibility referred to is exemplified by the people who have come to *believe* in God through individual, direct experiences. '*Believe*' is in italics, because the third possibility is about knowing and not belief. This experience mostly takes place in the context of a religion or a spiritual teaching.

Not all spiritual teachings or religions support the way of personal experience. Most Christian churches are primarily based on dogmas – which believers are supposed to believe in as facts – and do not focus on encouraging members to walk a personal path to individual experience. Nevertheless, Christianity can look back at a rich mystic tradition filled with valuable reports on the way leading to a direct experience of the spiritual reality.[152] To this day, many Christians walk the path to this personal experience.

Unlike Christian institutions, most Eastern religious schools – with Buddhism leading the way – attach great importance to the personal experience gained on a path of regularly practised meditation and much less to dogmatic teachings. This might be a major reason why many different Buddhist schools find followers in the West today. Yet, also Buddhism requires belief in the way – belief, in the sense of trust. In the Pāli Canon, Buddha says: '(...) any who have simply faith in me, simply love for me, are destined for heaven.' [153]

In summary, it can be said that the word 'belief', in the context of religion or spirituality, can be read in at least three different ways: Belief in the existence of God and the associated dogmas seen as facts, belief in the sense of trust and belief based on a direct experience of the divine or spiritual.

BELIEF AND EXPERIENCE

As discussed above, we are able to either believe in, or deny the existence or reality of the spiritual dimension of human life – a dimension which has been given many names but finally cannot be grasped by words alone. Whoever has experienced it can no longer deny this experience. We can also not deny the historical fact that many people have spoken of and reported on their personal experiences with this reality.

The direct experiencing of the divine, the numinous,[154] represents a dimension of human existence that – according to the accounts – lies beyond our perception, beyond thought and therefore also beyond speech. It has been given many names in the history of mankind, but ultimately remains nameless, because any attempt to substantiate it by means of words distorts it. This certainly is one reason why the second of the Ten Commandments reads: 'You shall not make for yourself a carved image'[155] – no object that you deify. Lao Tzu remarks that: 'Who knows does not speak',[156] and Meister Eckhart says: '[...] for words cannot give a name to any nature that is above her [soul]'.[157]

This is the reason why the canonical scriptures of various religions make frequent use of parables to describe this reality. Thus, we regularly read in the New Testament: 'The Kingdom of Heaven can be compared to (...)' followed by a parable. When Jesus is asked how the kingdom of God can be perceived, he answers with what it *isn't*: 'The kingdom of God is not coming in ways that can be observed, nor will they say, "Look, here it is!" or "There!" for behold, the kingdom of God is in the midst of you.'[158]

The namelessness of the divine is writ large in a central story of the Old Testament, where God speaks to Moses from a burning bush.[159] Moses repeatedly asks for a name, being afraid that nobody would believe that he has received a mission from God if he did not know God's name. He receives the following answer: 'I am who I am', meaning: nameless, without a name, with which man denominates an object that differs from other existing objects. A name, a thought, an image cannot capture what lies behind or beyond thought; where thought – as one of various ways that human life expresses itself – is contained.

The various descriptions of this experience of the spiritual reality reveal many differences that are connected to the times and cultural backgrounds within which they take place. Even within a religion itself, we can detect a certain transformation over time.[160] Since this reality eludes a description with words, reports on an epiphany – experiencing of the divine – can only ever be an approximation to it. They are themselves not this *encompassing*.[161] As illustrations, they are able to bring us closer to the experience of this dimension – if they are seen as signposts and not made into absolute spiritual reality itself.

Even though this divinity, this spiritual reality, cannot be put into words, the experiencing of it is *tangible* and effective. Man is overwhelmed by its grandeur and intensity and undergoes a change in his attitude.

The person who has experienced it regards the experiencing of spiritual reality no longer as an act of belief in its existence. The experiencing of it replaces belief with knowing.

However, it represents a personal experience that cannot be confirmed by anyone else. If I see the bus I have been waiting for, I know – based on my direct experience of the event in question – that the bus is on time today; I do not need to believe it. This refers to a different kind of knowledge than the personal experience of the numinous, since other people can confirm this event. I am therefore not dependent on my own subjective perception alone. Whilst experiencing the numinous, there is nobody who can confirm that my sensation is true. For nobody but me is directly experiencing it in the first place.

It raises the question of how a man or a woman can be sure that the experience of the spiritual reality, the numinous, is not a delusion – be it autosuggestion or hallucination. We are able to exclude a hallucination or delusion because the people who report on this experience are not mentally ill.[162] Most often, they display a more sober and realistic demeanour than the people around them.

There are at least two reasons why the person who has experienced it knows – without a single shadow of a doubt – that it represents a *real* experience of the numinous and not a delusion as a result of autosuggestion.

The *first* reason concerns the quality and the intensity of the experience. It is overwhelming, surpasses everything that the person has – to this point – experienced. Michael v. Brück describes the experience as follows: 'It is an intuitive, direct experience that does not need any verification from the surrounding.'[163]

When, for instance, Moses faces the burning bush, he has no doubt as to who is speaking to him[164] – even though he is not in a trance but completely rooted in reality. He does not delude himself with regards to his fellow men or the pharaoh. He accepts the fact that they will surely not believe the story of how God has charged him with a mission. This is why he asks for God's name, so that he might convince them.

We observe the same knowledge with Job: 'I am experiencing God's presence.' The book of Job recounts the story of the very struggle with the question of why God would let Job face such suffering. The question that the whole book deals with is why it is possible that people who live righteously and piously have to suffer so much more than scoundrels and villains who do not care for God.

The entirety of the Book of Job – up until the last five of the 42 chapters – revolves around this question. Job's friends – who visit him and pity him, but do not undergo the same suffering – attempt to explain to him that God is almighty, that he – as the creator and sole ruler – could do as he pleased. At the same time, they tell Job – in no uncertain terms – that his suffering indicates that he has done wrong in the eyes of God and advise him to ascertain what these ill deeds or thoughts were and ask God for forgiveness. For God would never punish a righteous man and if man suffers, then he does so as punishment. Job accepts and sees the omnipotence of God – which is depicted time and again in the book with impressive images and is contrasted to the impotence of man. Job realises, however, that the righteous and the pious are not necessarily better off than the godless. He himself serves as an example of it.

Because he has a fundamental trust in God, this question torments him. He calls upon God over and over and demands an answer, an explanation, in order to understand. While it is absolutely clear to him that he would never 'take God's name in vain', he nevertheless seeks to understand why it is possible for the way of the world to be so much different from what man is able to envision. In contrast to his friends who talk to him, he sees things as they are – not whitewashed by wishful thinking regarding a *just* God.

The direct experience of the presence of God gives Job an answer – while he does not receive an answer on the rational plane. 'I had heard of you by the hearing of the ear, but now my eye sees you.'[165] This serves as an answer for Job. The answer stems from the direct experience of the numinous. Job has no doubt as to who is speaking to him. He knows – he does not have to believe – that this is an encounter with God.

And when he says: 'Therefore I despise myself, and repent in dust and ashes',[166] it is an act of freedom and not duress. He does not surrender, nor does he reluctantly, bitterly or possibly masochistically accept his defeat. It is also not the fear that gives Job the answer he had been ever so desperately looking for. It is knowing by seeing: 'But now my eye sees you' – by directly experiencing the presence of God. It is comparable to someone who sees two spheres – one the size of a poppy-seed and the other the size of the construct enclosing the Eurosat rollercoaster at Europa-Park – a sphere with a diameter of 45 metres. The person is not coerced to realise that the second sphere is larger. He or she might not be able to judge differently upon seeing the two spheres, but the judgement itself represents an act of freedom.

In both examples, the exterior story – the story of what happens and can be perceived by an observer or a reader – is not necessarily discernible as the presence of the numinous. The personal experience is crucial to the quality of the event.

In the story of Moses, God appears in a burning bush. It might be odd – the bush is burning but not incinerated, which is why Moses approaches it – but most certainly not spectacular. Moses realises that God has appeared when God starts speaking to him. From that point on, he does not doubt the fact that he has had an encounter with the numinous.

With Job, God's answer – as it is recited in the final chapters of the book – includes almost nothing that hadn't already been expressed by Job or his friends. Virtually all the statements regarding the omnipotence and the grandeur of God can already be found in the same or a similar statement made during Job's arguments with his friends. The impact and undoubted certainty that God is speaking to Job does not stem from what is being put into words or what has happened viewed from the outside, but from the overwhelming experience of the presence of God. It is only immediately witnessed by Job, for only he – and not the friends – changes his attitude and knows that God has spoken to him. This experience transcends everything else – including his indescribable suffering – and answers all of his questions.

The tales of Moses and Job were used as two examples out of many, where the quality of the experience suffices to make sure that it represents an encounter with the numinous. Another example from the Bible can be found in the New Testament story about the conversion of Saul. Similar stories can be found in the canonical scriptures of other religions.

All tales that are rooted in various religions can nowadays be objected to based on the claim that they do not represent historically verified events. There is no steadfast proof that either Moses or Job actually existed. It has only been proven that these reports existed in written form before the beginning of our calendar. The lack of historical proof, nevertheless, does not lessen the value of these written traditions as examples or prototypes regarding the quality of this experience and the circumstances surrounding it.

We also find countless modern-day reports from women and men who have experienced this transpersonal dimension: Henri Le Saux,[167] Madeleine Delbrêl,[168] Simone Weil,[169] Ruben L.F. Habito,[170] Gangaji[171] and Eckhart Tolle,[172] to name but a few. With these people as well as the others, the quality and intensity of the experience leaves no doubt about the fact that they encountered the numinous. Terms such as *God*, *the one reality*, the *now*, the *all-reason-exceeding peace*, the *freedom*, the *unconditional, all-encompassing love*, have been used, even though the reports agree regarding the fact that this experience represents something that cannot be put into words.

Simone Weil writes in a letter to a priest: '(...) In this sudden possession of me by Christ, neither my senses nor my imagination had any part; I only felt in the midst of my suffering the presence of a love, like that which one can read in the smile on a beloved face. (...) I had never read any mystical works because I had never felt any call to read them. (...) God in his mercy had prevented me from reading the mystics, so that it should be evident to me that I had not invented this absolutely unexpected contact.'[173]

The *second* reason why this experience cannot be written off as delusion or autosuggestion but needs to be regarded as something genuine – as something appertaining to the human existence – is its repeated occurrence in different cultures and eras. Even though it cannot be put into words and remains thus ungraspable by objective knowledge, there is objective knowledge with regards to the historical fact that this experience is reported on in various parts of the world, cultures and eras – including today – and that these reports refer to the same reality. [174]

The knowledge of the spiritual reality

The reality of the spiritual dimension is not a question of belief to those who have experienced it. For them, it is knowledge based on direct experience. Notwithstanding the fact that other people cannot directly verify this personal experience, their stories are a matter of historical fact. This is why the spiritual dimension of human existence belongs to our cultural heritage, to our history as humans in the 21st century.

Meanwhile, the fact that its reality is considered to be proven – be it by means of direct experiences or as historical facts – and cannot be denied, does not reveal anything with regards to the cause of this experience.

Returning to the example of the red crayon – referred to in the part dealing with *Experience* – I am able to, with the aid of my other senses, examine the object and thereby detect whether the cause of my perception of the crayon is an image, a hologram or a crayon with which I am able to write. Certainly, there also are – even simply for practical reasons – limits to my ability to clarify all the circumstances that led to my experience of seeing the crayon on the table. It might not be possible for me to figure out who has put the crayon onto the table and what purpose that person pursued by doing so, who bought the crayon and where, what resources were used to manufacture the red colour, etc. Theoretically, I could investigate endlessly all the details that have led to my perception of the crayon.

Experiencing the spiritual dimension prevents an investigation into the possible causes leading to it, because it is – as an object and in turn as a concept – not graspable. While the experience itself may be part of a tangible reality, all suppositions regarding its cause and mode of formation remain mere hypotheses that ultimately cannot be verified.[175]

From a rational point of view, we cannot even be sure whether this experience requires the influence of a certain force – be it God, be it material or immaterial energy – that lies beyond our corporeal shells. Man could be inherently made to have the possibility of this experience within. This might, from the point of view of a *creative act,* even be more *challenging* than to create a human being influenced and steered by *God and the angels.* We do not know an answer and thereby experience the ultimate limit of our possibilities to explore the being of man by means of our reason. The fact that, in history, we encounter many different theories or teachings [176] confirms our inability to grasp the spiritual dimension by means of rational concepts.

The lack of knowledge of the causes and mechanisms that lead to the experience of the spiritual reality in no way diminishes its existential significance for human beings as individuals nor for mankind as a whole. It is the source of ethical and moral values and as such the sole dimension of our existence that bestows deep meaning – independent from external circumstances – and inner as well as interpersonal peace. It is the source of simply the most sublime virtue that we as humans are able to experience in this world: love – love as unconditional acceptance and compassion. It is therefore the only basis for a peaceful coexistence of human beings. [177]

This source is available to every man and woman through the spiritual path. This way is long and can lead through difficult phases. According to the Bible stories, Moses had to spend 40 years in the desert, and Job endured inconceivable suffering, before they were gifted with this experience. Even after the experience, life does not get any easier – or free from suffering – for the person who walks this path. Yet, life is imbued with meaning, peace and love that surpass everything else.

ADDITIONAL INFORMATION

ACKNOWLEDGEMENTS

In the poem 'The Other Shore,' Henri Le Saux writes: 'Man crosses to the other shore of his heart in the sacrament of the universe of mankind. Every man whom he meets and every being that he encounters is his ferryman, (...).'[178]

The book at hand was able to come into existence because I became aware of *the path to the other shore* as the most important purpose of my existence as a human being. I owe the fact that I set forth on it and walked this way to countless *ferrymen and ferrywomen.* The list of those I ought to give thanks to would fill yet another book. The ferrymen and ferrywomen who stood most steadfastly at my side as helpers are my parents, my siblings, my closest friends, my wife and my children: Helena, Bedřich, Lydia, Rut, Jana, Pavel, Maria, Honza, Ivo, Andi, Beatrix, Joan, Kaspar. The crucial inspiration to set forth on this path was drawn from 'Search for the Meaning of Life' by Willigis Jäger who was my spiritual teacher for many years. Reading his book, I was able to learn about object-free meditation as a spiritual path more than 20 years ago.

The fact that my texts could be published, I owe – as a non-writer – to the help of three eloquent people who tackled the proofreading and editing of the original German version with much patience and understanding: Monika Künzi, Martin Frischknecht and Eveline Blum who subedited some of these texts in their early stages – even before the thought of publishing them as a book arose. Peter Gottwald from Oldenburg and Andreas Tenzer from Cologne have been nice enough to read the first version of this book. Their very valuable suggestions have helped me in the definite arrangement of the texts at hand.

NOTES

---

[1] The term spiritual dimension or plane is used in this book to describe a dimension of our life where human beings are able to experience profound wisdoms of existential meaning. (See Appendix 1 for more)

[2] We do not know why we humans have this faculty. It quite likely has to do with the evolution of our mind. Our mind, with everything we experience of our external and internal world, asks the question of cause and effect. Our actions in everyday life are always accompanied by a reflection on the purpose and on the consequences of each act, either already experienced or anticipated. This *automatism*, of which in our daily life, we are only barely aware, is possibly the result of the evolutionary process and represents an ability of enormous importance to our lives and to our survival as human beings.

[3] Interestingly, a recent theory describes the origin of the cosmos as 'the sum of all [possible, i.e. infinite] histories'. Again, our mind is not able to provide us a definite answer here. See Stephen Hawking, Leonard Mlodinow. *The Grand Design*. Bantam Books 2012, p. 118

[4] Bertrand Russell. *A Free Man's Worship*. In *Mysticism and Logic*. Longmans Green, 1918. Cited here from Wikipedia (German) *Sinn des Lebens*. Accessed on 29.6.2017

[5] Ludwig Wittgenstein. Tractatus *Logico-philosophicus* 6.4312.

Ludwig Wittgenstein was one of the greatest logicians and philosophers of the 20th century. The *Tractatus Logico-philosophicus* was a seminal work in the origination of the school of analytical philosophy.

[6] An anthology of these descriptions in various cultures and religions can be found for example in: A. Huxley. *The Perennial Philosophy*. Chatto & Windus Ltd., London, 1957

[7] See note 1

[8] Lao Tzu writes, 'Who knows does not speak.' *Tao te Ching*, Chapter 56. Meister Eckehart says, 'Denn Worte vermögen keiner Natur, die oberhalb ihrer ist, einen Namen zu geben.' (English: '[...] for words cannot give a name to any nature that is above her [soul]'), Meister Eckehart. *Deutsche Predigten und Traktate*. Diogenes Verlag, Zürich, 1979, Predigt 17

[9] Bertrand Russell. *Wisdom of the West.* Macdonald London, 1959, p. 305

[10] See E. Fromm. *You Shall Be As Gods. A Radical Interpretation of the Old Testament and its Tradition.* First Fawcett Premier Edition, New York, 1969, Chapter 2: The Concept of God

[11] Jean Gebser. *Ursprung und Gegenwart.* DVA 1949 – 1953 und dtv, München, 1973. English translation: The Ever-Present Origin. Ohio University Press, 1985, 1991

[12] Ken Wilber. Sex, Ecology, Spirituality: The Spirit of Evolution. Shambhala Publications, 1994

[13] Eckhart Tolle. *A New Earth.* Penguin Books, 2005

[14] Willis Jäger. *Jenseits von Gott.* Verlag Wege der Mystik, 2012 (German: 'Es scheint, dass die Zeit eines kollektiven Erwachens angebrochen ist. Wir stehen an der Schwelle eines neuen Zeitalter, an der Schwelle einer Revolution. Wir entdecken, dass menschliche Wesen mehr sind als diese intellektuell geprägte Gestalt').

[15] The Dalai Lama says in a statement that is referred to in a book by a professor for religious studies, Michael von

Brück: 'Since love is at the core of all religions, we could speak of a universal religion of love.' (Transl. by the author) M. von Brück. *Buddhismus und Christentum*. Beck Verlag, München, 2000, p. 519 (German: 'Da aber Liebe wesentlich für alle Religionen ist, könnten wir von einer universalen Religion der Liebe sprechen.')

[16] John E. Coleman. *The Quiet Mind*. Rider, 1972, p. 94

[17] Psychoanalyst Hans-Joachim Maaz thus reasons that the predominant narcissistic disorder leads back to an unfulfilled experience of love for its own sake: 'Liebe um seiner selbst willen.' See J.-H. Maaz. *Die narzisstische Gesellschaft. Ein Psychogramm*. Beck Verlag, 2012

[18] Terry Eagleton. *The* Meaning *of Life*. Oxford University Press, 2007, p. 96

[19] Other examples are the statements of three renowned and influential philosophers of the 20th century: Russell, Camus and Wittgenstein.

Bertrand Russell writes in the prologue to his autobiography at the age of 84: 'Three passions, simple but overwhelmingly strong, have governed my life: the longing for love, the search for knowledge, and unbearable pity for the suffering of mankind.' (From: *What I Have Lived For*. Prologue to *The Autobiography of Bertrand Russell*,1967. Written on 25 July 1956.)

Albert Camus notes the following in his journal in June 1938: 'Misère et grandeur de ce monde: il n'offre point de vérités mais des amours. L'Absurdité règne et l'amour en sauve.' (Albert Camus. *Carnets I*. Édition Gallimard, Collection Folio, 2013, p. 102). English: 'The misery and greatness of this world: it offers no truths, but only objects for love. Absurdity is king, but love saves us from it.' (Translated by Hamish Hamilton)

Ludwig Wittgenstein writes in his journal in December 1948: 'The greatest happiness for a human being is love.' (Ludwig Wittgenstein. *Culture and Value*. Edited by G. H. von Wright. Blackwell Publishers, 1998, p. 87)

We find similar statements from other great philosophers, for example, Husserl, Bergson, Jaspers and Simone Weil. There are great men and women whom we admire because they acted according to the principle of love: Mahatma Gandhi, Martin Luther King, Nelson Mandela, Mother Teresa and others.

Thus, we find love – unconditional acceptance and compassion – as the highest value not only in the teachings of different religions but also in those of great philosophers and personalities. One could say that when a person looks deep enough for the meaning of life, he or she ends up at love. We cannot *understand* love and suffering but can perceive them as objective facts of utmost importance to human beings.

[20] See Stephen Hawking, Leonard Mlodinow. *The Grand Design*. Bantam Books 2012

[21] Karl Jaspers was interviewed by Thil Koch in a DRS radio programme in 1960.

[22] This is not specific to animals. Unicellular organisms are also known to obtain nutrients by eating other unicellular organisms.

[23] Incidentally, said egocentrism also provides the basis for the economic system of the current consumerist society – which in a way can be seen as a materialisation of the immaterial (composed of thoughts) egocentrism – that grows virtually ad infinitum.

[24] We of course do not know for sure whether there are living creatures capable of self-awareness and consciousness similar to what we observe in humans. In fact, we *cannot know* the inner life of an animal, as has been shown in an essay by the philosopher Thomas Nagel with the poignant title, '*What Is it Like to Be a Bat?*' (See: Thomas Nagel. *Mortal Questions*. Cambridge University Press 1991). Nonetheless, from the behaviours of the different species studied, we can deduce that the capacity for self-awareness and self-reflection as *highly* differentiated as in human beings is probably absent in them. Needless to say, we know that non-human creatures possess other faculties that we either lack, possess in poorly developed forms, or are entirely unaware of.

[25] There are many others who have walked this path and described it to their fellow men, from the Desert Fathers and various Buddhist and Sufi paths to contemporary spiritual teachers.

[26] Ken Wilber has poignantly formulated the fact that even these subjective experiences, in relation to their reality, are comparable with the experiences of the material world surrounding us. By means of a comparison, he formulates, 'If you want to know if the moons of Jupiter really exist, you must actually learn some of the principles of astronomy and then look through a telescope. Likewise, if you want to know whether the Zen state of *satori*, or enlightenment, really exists, you must learn something about Zen and then meditate, looking into the nature of your mind. Furthermore, he points out the fact that this approach – validation by means of empirical experiments and experiences – can in a way be seen as a scientific stance. This approach differs from the field of science concerned with the material world only in its inclusion of all levels and dimensions of our being and not merely the

material world. (See Ken Wilber et al. *Integral Life Practice*. Shambhala Publication Inc., 2008, p. 23)

[27] According to scientific research, the first evidence of life on our planet dates to about 4000 million years ago. Dodd, Matthew S.; Papineau, Dominic; Grenne, Tor; Slack, John F.; Rittner, Martin; Pirajno, Franco; O'Neil, Jonathan; Little, Crispin T. S. (1 March 2017). Evidence for early life in Earth's oldest hydrothermal vent precipitates. Nature. *543: 60–64.*

[28] Assuming that there is a creator – an intelligence – that guides these processes, the second of the two possibilities (no *extra*-terrestrial intervention) might make the act of creation even more challenging and, in this sense, does not contradict her/his *omnipotence*.

[29] Pascal's wager is an argument in philosophy that was devised by the seventeenth-century French philosopher, mathematician, and physicist Blaise Pascal (1623–62). It posits that humans bet with their lives that God either exists or does not.

Pascal argues that a rational person should live as though God exists and seek to believe in God. If God does actually exist, such a person will have only a finite loss (some pleasures, luxury, etc.), whereas they stand to receive infinite gains (as represented by eternity in heaven) and avoid infinite losses (eternity in hell).

Pascal's wager was based on the idea of the Christian God, though similar arguments have occurred in other religious traditions. The original wager was set out in section 233 of Pascal's posthumously published *'Pensées'* ("*Thoughts*"). These previously unpublished notes were assembled to form an incomplete treatise on Christian apologetics.

Historically, Pascal's wager was ground-breaking because it charted new territory in probability theory, marked the first formal use of decision theory, and anticipated future philosophies such as existentialism, pragmatism, and voluntarism. (Source: https://en.wikipedia.org/wiki/Pascal%27s_Wager (3 August 2017))

[30] Eckhart Tolle. *A New Earth*. Penguin Books, 2005

[31] See note 1.

[32] See Jonty Heaversedge, Ed Halliwell. *The Mindful Manifesto*. Hay House, Inc., 2010.

[33] Pali Canon; Majjhima Nikaya, M. 118. (XII,8) Ānāpānasati Sutta. English translation, e.g. Ñāṇamoli, Bhikkhu (trans.) & Bhikkhu Bodhi (ed.). The *Middle-length Discourses of the Buddha: A Translation of the Majjhima Nikāya*. Boston: Wisdom Publications, 2001.

[34] Frank Boccio. *Mindfulness Yoga*. Wisdom Publications, 1993.

[35] Anonymous. Ed. William Johnston. *The Cloud of Unknowing* and *The Book of Privy Counseling*. Image Book, 2005.

[36] Willigis Jäger. *Contemplation. A Christian Path*. Triumph Books, 1994.

[37] M. Williams et al. *The Mindful Way through Depression*. Guilford, 2007.

[38] M. von Brück. *Buddhismus und Christentum*. Beck Verlag, 2000, p. 519. Original German: 'Da aber Liebe wesentlich für alle Religionen ist, könnten wir von einer universalen Religion der Liebe sprechen' (Translated by author).

[39] John Lash. *The Yin of Tai-Chi*, 2007 ISBN 978-3-9523447, p. 20 and 27.

40 See Thich Nhat Hanh. *Going Home – Jesus and Buddha as Brothers*. Penguin Putnam Inc,, 2000.

41 See the Bible: Galatians 2:20.

42 Nowadays, we can find on the internet useful descriptions of how to sit. See the following:

http://www.insightmeditationcenter.org/books-articles/articles/postures-for-meditation/

http://www.wikihow.com/Sit-During-Meditation or

https://mindfulminutes.com/how-to-sit-for-meditation/

43 The fact that this experience happens to the meditating person and cannot be brought about by sheer will is emphasised both in Christianity and in other religions. This process is very vividly and impressively described in the book by Eugen Herrigel titled 'Zen in der Kunst des Bogenschiessens'. English: '*Zen in the Art of Archery*'.

44 Contemplation: Object-free meditation in Christian tradition. See Willigis Jäger. *Contemplation. A Christian Path*. Triumph Books, 1994.

45 www.sonnenhof-holzinshaus.de, www.benediktushof-holzkirchen.de

46 J. Krishnamurti. *Freedom from the Known*. Harper Collins Publishers, 1969.

47 Jon Kabat-Zinn. *Coming to Our Senses*. Hyperion, 2005.

48 Johannes Tauler. *Predigten*. Johannes Verlag, Einsiedeln – Trier, 1987.

Meister Eckhart. *The Complete Mystical Works of Meister Eckhart*. Translated and edited by Maurice O'C. Walshe. A Herder & Herder Book, The Crossroad Publishing Company New York, Sermon 21.

[49] Anonymous. Ed. William Johnston. *The Cloud of Unknowing* and *The Book of Privy Counseling*. Image Book, 2005.

[50] Willigis Jäger. *Search for the Meaning of Life*. Liguori/Triumph, 2003.

[51] Martin Laird. *Into the Silent Land. A guide to the Christian Practice of Contemplation*. Oxford University Press, 2006.

[52] Charlotte Joko Beck. *Everyday Zen*. Harper Collins, 2007.

Jack Kornfield. *The Path of Heart*. Rider Books, 2002.

[54] The term 'encompassing' or 'all-encompassing' originated with the philosopher Karl Jaspers. See Karl Jaspers. *Philosophy of Existence*. University of Pennsylvania Press, 1971.

[55] A group of blind men heard that a strange animal, called an elephant, had been brought to the town, but none of them knew what shape it was. They were curious and said, 'We must inspect and know it by touch, of which we are capable.' So, they sought it out, and when they found it, they groped about on it. The first person, whose hand landed on the trunk, said, 'This being is like a thick snake.' For another one whose hand reached its ear, it seemed like a kind of fan. For yet another person, whose hand was upon its leg, the elephant was a pillar like a tree-trunk. The blind man who placed his hand upon its side said, 'The elephant is a wall'. Another who felt its tail described it as a rope. The last felt its tusk, and stated that the elephant is that which is hard, smooth, and spear-like. (The parable originated in the ancient Indian subcontinent from where it was widely diffused. Source: https://en.wikipedia.org/wiki/Blind_men_and_an_elephant. (Viewed on 27 July 2017)

56 Source: Mahadev Desai. *The Gospel of Selfless Action or The (Baghavad) Gita According to Gandhi.* Navajivan Publishing House Ahmedabad-14. Ninth reprint, 1995, p. 308.

57 Source: Jack Kornfield, Gil Fronsdal. *Teachings of the Buddha.* Shambhala Publications, 2007, p. 92.

58 Socrates refers to it in Plato's Philebus 48c, and Phaedrus 229e as a saying of Delphi, and Louise Bourgeois cites it from Montaigne: 'When Montaigne said "connais-toi, toi même", he meant that the only useful approach to life is to know yourself. What you experience on the outside is actually what you experience on the inside.' (From Scott Lyon-Wall. *In Search of a State of Reason: Louise Bourgeois – Drawing and Sculpture.* In *Louise Bourgeois. Drawings and Sculpture.* Katalog Kunsthaus Bregenz, Verlag der Buchhandlung Walther König, Köln, 2002)

59 See note 24.

60 See note 57.

61 There are certainly other paths that lead to self-knowledge, e.g. philosophical reflections, psychology, psychotherapy, psychoanalysis or analytical psychology after Jung. By comparison, object-free meditation is an approach that devotes itself more directly to the aim of self-knowledge. It represents a direct self-observation in the present moment and not a (rational) analysis of past internal events.

62 The term *observer* (or observer of the observer respectively) and the notion that 'we are more than our thoughts, feelings, and corporeal sensations...' in this succinct phrasing were first chanced upon by the author in a book by Louise Reddemann: *Imagination als heilsame Kraft. Zur Behandlung von Traumafolgen mit ressourcenorientierten Verfahren,* Klett-Cotta, 2001, p.40

[63] Both 'I' and 'self' are used in this text to signify two different things: first, as my very own person with all my conscious and unconscious attributes, wishes, fears, desires, etc., and second, to signify an observer (and agent), through which I consciously perceive this world and act in it – an observer that eludes immediate observation. Here, 'I/self' is to be read with the second option in mind. Both meanings primarily stem from their linguistic applications and thereby do not represent definitively demarcated philosophical or psychological terms. It is therefore possible that, depending on the person, they are associated with different perceptions and demarcations. Since the path of object-free meditation represents an individual and personal experience that is different with each person, no impediment should arise from the exact meaning of the term 'I' being left to individual interpretation.

[64] In connection to Jungian psychotherapy, the shadow is defined as 'rejected and unaccepted aspects of personality that are repressed and form a compensatory structure' (Definition from Murray Stein. *C. G. Jung's Map of the Soul*. Open Court Publishing Company, 1998)

[65] There are countless books in the field of Christian, Buddhist and Islamic mysticism wherein this experience of the oneness, the One, is discussed.

[66] A path leading to the experience of the spiritual dimension (see note 1).

[67] Louise Reddemann, a well-known specialist in the field of psychotherapeutic medicine and author, speaks of love as the 'deep origin of being' (see *Eine Reise von 1.000 Meilen beginnt mit dem ersten Schritt,* Herder, 2008, p.124).

[68] John E. Coleman. *The Quiet Mind.* Rider, 1971, p.94.

[69] Also see Part III.

[70] Whenever 'I' is used in this text, neither the author nor another person are directly referred to. It is used to underline the individual nature of the events described.

[71] Or that Leo Tolstoy describes in his short yet impressive work entitled '*A Confession*'.

[72] Angelus Silesius: *The Cherubinic Wanderer.*

[73] This is why the Dalai Lama says, 'Since love is at the core of all religions, we could speak of a universal religion of love.' (M. von Brück. *Buddhismus und Christentum.* Beck Verlag, München, 2000, p. 519) (Translated by the author)

[74] The term 'das Umgreifende/Allumgreifende' (Encompassing or all-encompassing) originates with Karl Jaspers (see e.g., Karl Jaspers. *Philosophical Faith and Revelation. Harper & Row, 1967*).

[75] 'God is love, and whoever abides in love abides in God, and God abides in him.' (1 John 4:16) English Standard Version.

[81] This chapter is written from the perspective of a person whose religious belief is based on the Christian canonical texts (i.e., the Bible and in particular the New Testament).

[82] This by no means seeks to indicate that for the people who have heard this message and are walking on the path, a community is of no importance.

[83] The word *God* is used since it is the denomination used in the Bible and in turn in Christianity for the *eternal, absolute being* that man is not able to grasp with his senses and mind – but, as a Christian, turns to in prayer. The various ecclesiastical dogmas that deal with the description of God are not touched by this notion.

[84] See the chapter titled '*Practising Object-free meditation*'.

[85] See Willigis Jäger. *Contemplation. A Christian Path.* Triumph Books 1994; or Thomas Merton. *New Seeds of Contemplation.* Shambhala Publications, 2003.

[86] What exactly the righteousness of God is can be read in the Bible, most notably in the *Sermon on the Mount* in the fifth chapter of the Gospel according to Matthew.

[87] Louise Reddeman. *Eine Reise von 1000 Meilen beginnt mit dem ersten Schritt. Seelische Kräfte entwickeln und fördern.* Herder Verlag, 2008, p. 124. (Translated by the author)

Prof. Dr. med. Louise Reddemann lives in Germany. She is a well-known specialist in the field of psychotherapeutic medicine with a focus on trauma therapy and is a writer of numerous specialist books.

[88] Jon Kabat Zinn. *Coming to our senses. Healing ourselves and the world through mindfulness.* Hyperion New York, 2005, p. 78.

Jon Kabat-Zinn is a retired professor at the University of Massachusetts Medical School in Worcester. He teaches mindfulness meditation, in order to help people to deal with stress, fear and illnesses. He is the author of several books and a pioneer in the application of the practice of mindfulness in medicine.

[89] Larry Rosenberg. *Breath by Breath.* Shambhala Publications 2004, p. 194.

Larry Rosenberg is a Buddhist spiritual teacher at the Cambridge Insight Meditation Center in Massachusetts, USA, which he founded over 30 years ago.

[90] John E. Coleman. *The Quiet Mind.* Rider 1971, p. 94.

Jiddu Krishnamurti was one of the most influential spiritual teachers of the last century. Unlike most other teachers, he greatly emphasised freedom from all religious teachings and concepts. To him, they represent beliefs and images that impede a clear view of the spiritual dimension of human existence.

[91] Kabir. *murall bajat akhay,d saddye.* In *Kabir's poems. Translated by Rabindranath Tagore.* Macmillan and Co., Limited, 1915, p. 56.

Kabir was an Indian mystic who lived in the 15th century. He believed that man should not live according to the Quran or the Vedas, but should attempt to either emulate the ideals of the Sahaj (a path of the heart-meditation) or find a simple, close-to-nature path to God. He rejected the caste system of the orthodox Hindus.

[92] *1 John 4: 16,* English Standard Version.

[93] See note 62.

[94] 'Absolute' (from the Latin word *absolutus* 'released') means 'independent from all influences'.

[95] Brian Daizen Victoria. *Zen at war.* Rowman & Littlefield Publishers, 2006.

[96] This does not mean that a careful inspection concerning the authenticity of these reports and the integrity of these authors is not necessary. Sadly, on the growing market of esotericism, many things are offered based on mere commercial interests.

[97] See also the Appendix: *Believing and Knowing.*

[98] The fact is that many people who learn of the message of the spiritual path do not set forth on it. This also happened during the times of Buddha and Christ, as the following text shows (it depicts a parable told by Jesus): 'A sower went out to sow. And as he sowed, some seeds fell along the path, and the birds came and devoured them. Other seeds fell on rocky ground, where they did not have much soil,

and immediately they sprang up, since they had no depth of soil, but when the sun rose they were scorched. And since they had no root, they withered away. Other seeds fell among thorns, and the thorns grew up and choked them. Other seeds fell on good soil and produced grain, some a hundredfold, some sixty, some thirty.' Matthew 13:3–8 English Standard Version.

99 See Karl R. Popper: *In Search of a Better World.* Taylor & Francis Ltd., 1995.

100 They can be found in the canonical scripts of many religions: Christian, Buddhist, Jewish or others. (The three religions named are personally known to the author.)

101 See note 1.

102 'Regardless of whether or not we belong to a religion, we all have a fundamental and profoundly human wellspring of ethics within ourselves. We need to nurture that shared ethical basis. (...) More integral than religion is our fundamental human spirituality – that is the affinity we humans have for love, benevolence, and affection – no matter what religion we belong to.' (The Dalai Lama and Franz Alt. *An Appeal to the World. Ethics are More Important than Religion.* Benevento, 2015)

103 Matthew 5:8 English Standard Version.

104 Gangaji. *The Diamond in Your Pocket.* Sounds True Inc., 2004.

105 See Chapter: *Practising Object-free meditation.*

106 The simile of the glasses, signifying our bias with regard to our world and with ourselves, is very old. The author chanced upon it for the very first time in the book *The Labyrinth of the World and Paradise of the Heart* by John Amos Comenius, originally published in Czech in 1623.

[107] There are phases of life – puberty and adolescence for instance – when people rebel against the rules of conduct imposed on us by our upbringing. This mostly constitutes another pair of *glasses* that the youth has taken to wearing, influenced by socialising with other youths. Quite commonly, the distortion of the view – in such phases of revolt – caused by the pressure to conform to the rules of the group of coevals, even increases in comparison to *well-adjusted* people.

[108] Z. V. Segal, J. M. G. Williams, J. D. Teasdale. *Mindfulness-based Cognitive Therapy for Depression.* Guilford, 2012.

[109] In connection to the Jungian psychotherapy the shadow is defined as 'rejected and unaccepted aspects of personality that are repressed and form a compensatory structure'. (Definition from: Murray Stein. *C. G. Jung's Map of the Soul.* Open Court Publishing Company, 1998)

[110] Jon Kabat Zinn. *Coming to our senses. Healing Ourselves and the World Through Mindfulness.* Hyperion New York, 2005, p. 84.

[111] In this context, Zen Masters use the lunar phases as similes: the first stage is the fifteen days until the full moon, and the second, the fifteen days after the full moon. This second stage is crucial for the integration of the spiritual values in everyday life. (See Ruben Habito. *Living Zen, Loving God.* Wisdom Publications, Boston, 2004, p. 45)

[112] See e.g., J. Krishnamurti. *Freedom from the Known.* Harper Collins Publishers, 1969.

[113] *I/self* is used in this text in order to signify two different things: firstly, as my very own person with all my conscious and unconscious attributes, wishes, fears, desires, etc.; secondly, to signify an observer (and agent), through which I consciously perceive and act in this world,

an observer who eludes immediate observation. In this chapter, *I/self* is to be read with the first option in mind. Both meanings are primarily based on the words' linguistic applications and do not represent definitively demarcated philosophical or psychological terms. It is therefore possible that they are associated with different perceptions and demarcations for different people. Since the path of object-free meditation represents an individual personal experience different with each person, it should not be impedimental for the exact meaning of the term *I/self* to be left to individual interpretation.

[114] A story from Zen Buddhism tells the tale of an old Chinese monk who, after many years of meditation, decided to retreat to a hut on the mountain and to stay there until he finished his practice. On the way up the mountain he met an old man walking down, carrying a big bundle. The old man asked the monk where he was going and the monk answered: "I am going to the top of the mountain to sit and either get enlightened or die". The old man let go of his bundle, and it dropped to the ground. In that moment, the monk was enlightened. "You mean it is that simple; just to let go and not grasp anything!" Then the newly enlightened monk looked back at the old man and asked, "So now what?" In answer, the old man reached down and picked up the bundle again and walked off toward town. (Abridged from: Jack Kornfield. *The Path of Heart*. Rider Books, 2002, p. 154)

[115] 'And he said to all, "If anyone would come after me, let him deny himself and take up his cross daily and follow me".' (Luke 9:23 English Standard Version*)*

[116] Our self has been conditioned by evolution and by the culture within which we have grown up to the extent that it can hardly be bettered within a couple of years by a training programme.

117 This is where all concepts of the various spiritual paths meet.

118 Jesus himself said: 'learn from me, for I am gentle and lowly in heart' (Matthew 11:29) English Standard Version.

119 Karl Popper. In Search of a Better World. Routledge, 1994, p. 199.

Another great philosopher and Nobel laureate, Bertrand Russell, writes in his essay "Mysticism and Logic": *The greatest men who have been philosophers have felt the need both of science and of mysticism.* (Bertrand Russell. *Mysticism and Logic and Other Essays.* George Allen & Unwin Ltd, London, 1959).

120 *A. Huxley: The Perennial Philosophy*, Chatto & Windus Ltd., London, 1957.

121 M. von Brück. *Buddhismus und Christentum*. Beck Verlag, München, 2000, p. 519 (German: 'Da aber Liebe wesentlich für alle Religionen ist, könnten wir von einer universalen Religion der Liebe sprechen.') English translation by the author.

122 1 John 4:16 English Standard Version.

123 Ludwig Wittgenstein. *Licht und Schatten*. Herausgegeben von Ilse Somavilla. Haymon Verlag 2014, p. 44.

124 Whenever 'I' is used in this text, neither the author nor another person are directly referred to. It is used to underline the individual nature of the events described.

125 John E. Coleman. *The Quiet Mind*. Rider, 1971, p. 94.

126 *The Complete Mystical Works of Meister Eckhart.* Translated by Maurice O'C. Walshe. The Crossroad Publishing Company, 2009.

[127] *Johannes Tauler: Predigten.* Johannes Verlag, Einsiedeln – Trier, 1987.

[128] Anonymous. *The Cloud of Unknowing.* Edited by James Walsh. Paulist Press, 1981.

[129] *The Complete Mystical Works of Meister Eckhart.* Translated by Maurice O'C. Walshe. The Crossroad Publishing Company, 2009, Sermon 4: p. 56–57

[130] *The Cloud of Unknowing.* Edited by James Walsh. Paulist Press, 1981, p. 252.

[131] Shunryu Suzuki. *Zen Mind, Beginner's mind.* Shambhala Publications, 2011, p. 100.

[132] Or the Epiphany, Nirvana, the union with Atman, as it is called in Buddhism and Hinduism.

[133] Paul Tillich, a theologian and philosopher, writes: 'Religion [God] is the experience of the unconditioned and this means the experience of absolute reality founded on the experience of absolute nothingness. One experiences the nothingness of entities, of values, the nothingness of the personal life. Wherever this experience has brought one to the nothingness of an absolute radical No, there it is transformed into an experience, no less absolute, of reality, into a radical Yes.' (Victor Nuovo. *Visionary Science: A Translation of Paul Tillich's 'On the Idea of a Theology of Culture' with an Interpretive Essay.* Detroit: Wayne State University Press, 1987, p. 24). (German: «Religion [Gott] ist Erfahrung des Unbedingten und das heisst Erfahrung schlechthinniger Realität auf der Grundlage der Erfahrung schlechthinniger Nichtigkeit; es wird erfahren die Nichtigkeit des Seienden, die Nichtigkeit der Werte, die Nichtigkeit des persönlichen Lebens; wo diese Erfahrung zum absoluten, radikalen Nein geführt hat, da schlägt sie um in eine ebenso absolute Erfahrung der Realität, in ein

radikales Ja.» (Paul Tillich. *Ausgewählte Texte.* Herausgegeben von Christian Danz, Werner Schüssler und Erdmann Sturm. Walter de Gruyter 2008, p. 30).

[134] Arriving at this experience can also be much more painful – through dramatic life events that lead me to utter exasperation, through loss of what is dearest to me.

[135] John of the Cross, St. *Dark Night of the Soul.* Christian Classics Ethereal Library, 1959.

[136] *The Complete Mystical Works of Meister Eckhart.* Translated by Maurice O'C. Walshe. The Crossroad Publishing Company, 2009, p. 491.

[137] John 3:8 English Standard Version.

[138] 'One asks oneself then whether it is possible to come upon this thing without inviting, without waiting, without seeking or exploring - just for it to happen like a cool breeze that comes in when you leave the window open? You cannot invite the wind but you must leave the window open, which doesn't mean that you are in a state of waiting; that is another form of deception. It doesn't mean you must open yourself to receive; that is another kind of thought.' Jiddu Krishnamurti. *Freedom from the Known.* Harper Collins Publisher, 2008, p. 122.

[139] Matthew 16:24 English Standard Version.

[140] From: Ayya Khema. *Was du suchst, ist in deinem Herzen.* Herder Verlag 2007, p. 18. (German: «Wenn wir uns nicht wenigstens zeitweilig hingeben können, ist es unmöglich, mit dem Denken aufzuhören ... Aber in dem Moment, wo wir gewillt sind, uns hinzugeben, wird Meditation möglich.» English translation by the author).

[141] Mahadev Desai. *The Gospel of Selfless Action or The (Baghavad) Gita According to Gandhi.* Navajivan Publishing House Ahmedabad-14. Ninth reprint 1995, p. 306.

---

[142] See also Part III.

[143] Matthew 22:37 English Standard Version.

[144] Simone Weil. *Selected Essays, 1934 – 1943*. Translated by Richard Rees. Wipf & Stock Pyblishers, Eugene, Oregon, 2017, p. 219.

[145] ibid, p. 220. As a philosopher Simone Weil formulates her concept in a language that is disconnected from any religious teaching. It does not, however, contradict the Christian teaching, because Christianity was very important to her, even though she could not join the official Church due to its dogmatic doctrine and attitude.

[146] The Dalai Lama and Franz Alt. *An Appeal to the World. Ethics are More Important than Religion*. Benevento, 2015.

[147] As in sitting meditation, it is also important to set an alarm clock for this time window so we can let go of our conscious or subconscious monitoring of time during the session.

[148] Blaise Pascal. *Pascal's Pensées*. E: P. Dutton & Co., Inc., 1958, p. 66 (Paperback edition). See also note 29.

[149] In his book *Stories of Mr. Keuner* Bertolt Brecht relates the following story: 'A man asked Mr. K. whether there is a God. Mr. K. said: "I advise you to consider whether, depending on the answer, your behaviour would change. If it would not change, then we can drop the question. If it would change, then I can at least be of help to the extent that I can say, you have already decided: you need a God."' (City Lights Books, 2001, p. 14)

[150] Interestingly enough, Hans Küng in his book *What I Believe* speaks out – albeit not directly – in favour of this. When he is asked: 'Have you ever doubted the Existence of

God?' he clearly answers that he has never doubted it (p. 85). However, when he speaks about his own death in the Chapter *Ars moriendi*, he says: 'But what if I am wrong and I do not enter God's eternal life but nothingness?' (p. 181). One needs to ask whether he has really never doubted God, when he adds at the end of the book that he also might be wrong. (Hans Küng. *What I believe.* Continuum International Publishing Group, 2010)

151 When speaking of belief with regards to trust and not religious conviction, the English language uses *faith* and French *foi*. German does not know this difference.

152 An overview can be found in: Gerhard Ruhbach und Josef Sudbrack, Herausgeber. *Grosse Mystiker. Leben und Wirken.* Verlag C.H. Beck München, 1984.

153 Majjhima Nikaya, 22. Cited from: *The Life of Buddha According to the Pali Canon.* Translation from the Pali and selection of material by Bhikkhu Nanamoli. Buddhist Publication Society, Kandy Sri Lanka 1992

154 The Judeo-Christian tradition often uses the word *epiphany* in relation to this experience of the encounter with the spiritual dimension.

155 Exodus 20:4. English Standard Version.

156 Lao Tzu. *Tao te Ching*, Chapter 56.

157 Meister Eckhart. *The Complete Mystical Works of Meister Eckhart.* Translated and Edited by Maurice O'C. Walshe. A Herder & Herder Book, The Crossroad Publishing Company New York, Sermon 21.

158 Luke 17:20-21. English Standard Version.

159 Exodus Chapter 3.

160 See for instance: E. Fromm. *You Shall Be As Gods. A Radical Interpretation of the Old Testament and its*

Tradition. First Fawcett Premier Edition, New York, 1969, Chapter 2: The concept of God.

[161] This term originated with Karl Jaspers. (see Karl Jaspers. *Philosophical Faith and Revelation.* Harper & Row, 1967)

[162] Psychological illnesses which lead to hallucinations or religious delusions are most often psychoses such as schizophrenia.

[163] Michael von Brück. *Was ist Wahrheit? Zum Begriff der Wahrheit in europäischen und indischen Traditionen.* Translation by the author. Essay published on: https://www.tibet.de/ fileadmin/pdf/tibu/2007/tibu083-2007-28-mb-wahrheit.pdf, viewed on 23.07.2017

[164] 'And Moses hid his face, for he was afraid to look at God.' Exodus 3:6. English Standard Version.

[165] Job 42:5. English Standard Version.

[166] Job 42:6. English Standard Version.

[167] Henry le Saux. *Zum anderen Ufer. Die Spiritualität der Upanishaden.* Eugen Diederichs Verlag, 1994.

[168] Madeleine Delbrêl (1904-1964) is called 'Mystic of the street.' She describes the experience at the end of a very painful process as follows: 'A radical change, encounter with the living God, experiencing a love that left no choice, an overwhelming being enraptured to God.' Before undergoing the painful process that preceded this experience, she was a confident atheist. Cited from M. Delbrêl. *Gott einen Ort sichern.* Verlagsgemeinschaft topos plus, Kevelaer, 2013. (Translated by the author)

[169] Simone Weil. *Spiritual Biography.* In *Waiting for God.* Harper Perennial Modern Classics, 2009.

[170] Ruben L.F. Habito. *Living Zen, Loving God.* Wisdom Publications, Boston, 2004.

[171] Gangaji. *The Diamond in Your Pocket.* Sounds True Inc., 2004.

[172] Eckhart Tolle. *The Power of Now.* Hodder & Stoughton, 2011.

[173] Simone Weil. *Spiritual Biography.* In *Waiting for God.* Harper Perennial Modern Classics, 2009.

[174] A summary of these descriptions in various cultures and religions can be found in: Aldous Huxley. *The Perennial Philosophy.* Chatto & Windus Ltd., London, 1946 or in the comments by Mahadev Desai in *The Gospel of Selfless Action or The Gita according to Gandhi.* Dry Bones Press, Inc. Roseville, CA, 2000.

[175] This is perhaps also what Jesus meant when he says to Nicodemus: 'The wind blows where it wishes, and you hear its sound, but you do not know where it comes from or where it goes. So it is with everyone who is born of the Spirit' (John 3:8 English Standard Version).

[176] Starting with the Vedas and the Jewish religion, through Buddhism, Taoism, Christianity, Islam, to the Mormons, A Course in Miracles, etc.

[177] In his book *The Meaning of Life*, Terry Eagleton sees *love* as the (only) possibility to reconcile our pursuit of individual fulfilment – specific to humankind – with the fact that man can only exist as a social being. Terry Eagleton. *The Meaning of Life.* Oxford University Press, 2007, p. 96.

In his foreword to the book *Peace is Every Step* by Thich Nhat Hanh, the Dalai Lama writes: 'Although attempting to bring about world peace through the internal

transformation of individuals is difficult, it is the only way.
Wherever I go, I express this (...)' (Thich Nhat Hanh. *Peace
is Every Step: The Path of Mindfulness in Everyday Life.*
Bantam Books, 1992)

[178] Henry le Saux. *Zum anderen Ufer. Die Spiritualität der
Upanishaden.* Eugen Diederichs Verlag, 1994, p. 30.
(Translated by the author)

www.ingramcontent.com/pod-product-compliance
Lightning Source LLC
LaVergne TN
LVHW091044170726
843494LV00001B/53